70 Healthy Slow Cooker Recipes

The Mediterranean Diet

Copyright © by: Kate Rosetti 2014

Copyright © by: Gold-Collier Publishing Company 2014

ISBN-13:978-1493778997

All cover photo images provided under Creative Commons license.

DISCLAIMER

These ideas and suggestions written by Kate Rosetti are provided as general educational information only and should not be construed as medical advice or care. All matters regarding your health require supervision by a personal physician or other appropriate health professional familiar with your current health status. Always consult your personal physician before making any dietary or exercise changes. Kate Rosetti and Gold-Collier Publishing Company disclaim any liability or warranties of any kind arising directly or indirectly from use of this information. If any medical problems develop, always consult your personal physician. Only your physician can provide you medical advice.

Throughout this document are links to external sites. These external sites contain information created and maintained by other individuals and organizations and are provided for the user's convenience. Kate Rosetti and Gold-Collier Publishing Company do not control nor can they guarantee the accuracy, relevance, timeliness, or completeness of this information. Neither is it intended to endorse any view expressed nor reflect its importance by inclusion in this site.

Contents

Welcome 1

How to Choose a Slow Cooker 3

How to Use a Slow Cooker 5

Soup: 10

    A Note about Lentils: 11

    Moroccan Red Lentil Soup 13

    Lentil Spinach Soup 16

    Curried Lentil Soup 18

    The Easiest Lentil Soup I Know 21

    Basque Black Bean Soup 23

    Vegetable Soup 27

    Borscht 31

    Mushroom - Barley Soup 35

    Barley Vegetable Soup 38

    Tuscan Bean and Kale Soup 41

    Golden Mushroom Soup 44

    Vegetarian Split Pea Soup 47

    Fasolatha (Greek Bean Soup) 50

    Spinach-Vegetable Soup 53

    Seafood Stew 55

    Italian Seafood and Fennel Stew 59

Beans: 63

    White Beans with Sun-Dried Tomatoes 63

    White Beans with Pesto 66

- Basil Pesto 69
- White Bean and Cabbage Soup 71
- White Beans Squash Kale and Olive Stew 74

Seafood: 77
- Greek Shrimp and Feta Cheese 77
- Atum Basco com Batatas e Pimentões Vermelho 80
  - Basic Polenta 83
- Citrus Salmon 89
- Salmon with Mango Avocado Salsa 92
  - Mango Avocado Salsa 94
- Salmon with Asparagus 96
- Shrimp Marinara 100
- Foil Wrapped Lemon Pepper Sole with Asparagus 103
- Slow Cooker Chicken and Shrimp 106
- Poached Swordfish with Lemon-Parsley Sauce 109
- Easy Cheesy Salmon Loaf 113
- Slow-Cooker Halibut Stew 116
- Salmon and Green Beans 118
- Slow Cooker Poached Salmon 120
  - Horseradish Sauce 122
- Vegetable Ragout with Cornmeal Crusted Halibut Nuggets 123
- Salmon with Lemon and Green Olive Sauce 127
- Salmon with Dill and Shallots 130
  - Thyme-Roasted Sweet Potatoes 133

Vegetarian: 136
    Vegetarian Stuffed Peppers 136
    Tex-Mex Lentils..140
    North African Squash-Eggplant Casserole 142
    Easy Ratatouille..145
    Mediterranean Eggplant...148
    Slow Cooker Rotisserie Style Chicken 151
    Chicken with 40 Cloves of Garlic Slow Cooker Style 154
    Lemon Chicken with Broccoli......................................157
        All Purpose Seasoning Mix....................................160
    Super Easy Chicken Cacciatore 162
    Mediterranean Chicken with Wine and Olives 165
        How To Cook Spaghetti Squash: 166
    Greek Chicken and Vegetable Casserole 168
    Herbed Chicken Breasts with White Beans..........171
    Peru com Porto, Frutas e Azeitonas.........................173
    Vermont Style Sweet and Tangy Turkey Thighs.................176
    Greek Style Turkey Breast...178
        All Purpose Greek Seasoning Blend 181
    Turkey Breast White Beans and Artichokes........183

Beef:..185
    Mediterranean Pot Roast in Red Wine Sauce......185
    Mediterranean Pot Roast with Vegetables...........188
    Moroccan Beef Tagine 191

Ras El Hanout 194

Greek Beef and Eggplant 196

Mediterranean Beef Stew with Olives and Sun-Dried Tomatoes 199

Pork: 202

Tuscan Pork and White Beans 202

Pork Mediterranean Style 205

Easy White Bean Cassoulet 209

Orange Pork Roast 212

Pork Roast Sweet Potatoes and Onions 216

Dessert: 219

Indian Pudding 220

Lemon Pudding Cake 223

Slow Cooker Baked Apples 225

Brown Rice Pudding 228

Stewed Prunes 230

Welcome

Welcome to "*70 Slow Cooker Recipes For The Mediterranean Diet*". It's actually 77 but who's counting! This is intended as a companion volume to *"The Mediterranean-Diet: An-Eating-Plan-Healthy For A Healthy Life*" but is also written as a standalone book.

Don't know much about the Mediterranean Diet? Wonder what it is? The Mediterranean Diet isn't really a diet in the sense that we've come to define the word diet. The Mediterranean Diet is a lifestyle plan for living a healthy life. It is based on studies which were conducted on people who reside on the shores of the Mediterranean Sea. There isn't "a" Mediterranean diet per say because Greeks eat differently from Italians, who eat differently from the French and Spanish but they share many common threads in their dietary habits and lifestyles.

Studies show that the folks in the countries bordering the Mediterranean Sea live longer and suffer less than most Americans from cancer and cardiovascular ailments. The formula for their good health seems to be an active lifestyle coupled with weight control, and a diet low in red meat, sugar, and saturated fat and high in produce, nuts, and other healthful foods.

The Mediterranean diet focuses on the consumption of fruits, vegetables, whole grains, beans, nuts, legumes, olive oil, and flavorful herbs and spices.

Eating fish and seafood at least a couple of times a week is encouraged as is enjoying poultry, eggs, cheese, and yogurt in moderation. On the Mediterranean eating plan sweets and red meat are reserved for special occasions.

If you want, you can top it off with a glass or two of red wine, but remember to stay physically active, and you're set.

As you may or may not know from reading *"[The Mediterranean-Diet: An-Eating-Plan for A-Healthy Life](#)"* I live this way and have for many years. The one major difference in my approach is that I don't eat any meat and haven't for 25 years or so. I think making this lifestyle choice has been beneficial for me as my weight has never fluctuated more than a few pounds throughout my adult life. I also don't suffer from any of the diseases and conditions such as digestive disorders, arthritis, heart disease, high blood pressure, or any of the other conditions found all too often in this society.

So, with that being said, let's get down to business and learn how to teach our slow cookers to embrace the Mediterranean lifestyle.

How to Choose a Slow Cooker

If you're thinking about purchasing a slow cooker, here are a few steps to help you find the model that suits your needs.

1. .Choose the right size. You can buy tiny slow cookers and extremely large slow cookers.
- The size of your family will be what determines which size is best for you. Also consider that most slow cooker recipes are written for a 6 quart unit. I find this size best suited to my needs because it provides me with enough leftovers to freeze. I also have a 4 quart slow cooker and I don't use it nearly as often as the larger one. When choosing a slow cooker, just remember that they operate most efficiently when 3/4 full and if they contain less, will cook food too quickly. If you think you may need a small slow cooker from time to time, consider purchasing two of different sizes or choose one with different sized inserts.

2. .Look at heat settings. Almost every slow cooker will have a low and high setting, but
- some models also have a keep warm setting. If your family eats at different times, this is an important feature to consider. It's also a nice feature if you plan on using your slow cooker at parties.

3\. Choose a model that has a removable insert. A removable insert makes clean up easier because you can remove it and wash it without worrying about damaging the electrical components.

There's also another reason for choosing a model with a removable insert and that is it's easier to fit in your fridge. Why would you want to do this? It saves precious time in the morning if you fill your slow cooker insert with your recipe at night so when you're getting ready for your day, all you have to do is remove the insert from the fridge and pop it in the slow cooker. This is a real time saver on busy mornings.

4\. It doesn't matter what I'm buying, I always read reviews. Reviews will save you from throwing money down the drain. No matter how perfect a product seems to be in a description, reading reviews from real people will make you aware of any problems only people who have owned the product can tell you about.

How to Use a Slow Cooker

If you have a busy schedule and prefer to cook at home, a slow cooker just might fit the bill. These appliances make coming home to a well cooked meal convenient for you if you're gone all day.

Slow cookers have evolved since their invention to include not only designs that are more stylish but include practical improvements such as built in timers and more temperature settings. Even with the improved functions built into today's slow cookers, the intended use remains the same.

I hope you find these suggestions on how to use your slow cooker useful:

1. Find a place on your kitchen counter which is near an outlet. Clear away the junk on your counter so the slow cooker has at least 6 inches (15.2 cm) space between it and any other appliances, food wrappers, walls or other surfaces. The slow cooker does not get hot enough to burn your countertop, but it can damage other surfaces that rest against it or near it.

2. Prep your food for your slow cooker recipe before you fill your slow cooker. Chop, slice or dice vegetables as directed by the recipe.

Do this ahead of time, even the night before, to speed up the assembling process. Remember to trim fat and gristle from meat.

3. If time allows, brown meat and sauté vegetables to add more flavor to your recipe, if the recipe calls for this step. This step can be omitted if you don't have time for it but it's to your advantage to take the time to do it.

4. Season your meat and vegetables. If your recipe doesn't require you to season the meat or vegetables before adding them to the slow cooker, just measure them out in advance so you'll remember what you need to add when it comes time to fill your slow cooker

5. Put the food and seasonings in the slow cooker. Layer food into your slow cooker in the order listed in your recipe unless you're making a soup. It doesn't matter which order soup ingredients go in the slow cooker. It's all going to get stirred together anyway.

Some recipes suggest layering food into your slow cooker in a specific order because some areas of your slow cooker get hotter and stay hotter for longer periods of time.

6. Pour liquid into the slow cooker. Make sure you have enough liquid to fill it half to three-quarters full after the liquid is added to the food contents.

Place the lid on your slow cooker. If the lid has any gaps or is loose, put a layer of aluminum foil under the cover, wrapping the top of the slow cooker tightly. It's important for the lid to fit tightly for your slow cooker to be efficient.

7. Turn your slow cooker on. Select the proper setting. Choose the low setting if you want your recipe to cook for 8 to 10 hours. The low setting allows a slower warm up period, which often results in more tender meat and vegetables. Select the high setting to cook your meal for 4 to 6 hours.

8 No peeking! Allow your food to cook and leave the lid on so heat doesn't escape.
- Peeking means that every time you lift the lid the slow cooker has to recover from its heat loss which means your food will take longer to cook. Also, resist the urge to stir halfway through the cooking time. Stirring is unnecessary.

9 Add extra ingredients at the end. If your recipe calls for pasta, add it during the last
- 30 minutes of cooking. Pasta cooks more quickly and becomes mushy if left in the slow cooker too long. It will also become mushy if you put it in a cool slow cooker.

If your recipe calls for cornstarch, place the cornstarch in a small dish, add a couple tablespoons of cold liquid, stir to dissolve and add to your slow cooker 20 to 30 minutes before your meal is ready. Don't mix the cornstarch up well in advance. It will get hard and be impossible to stir.

10. Add quick-cooking vegetables such as broccoli, cauliflower and corn during the last hour of cooking.

Add seafood not more than 60 minutes before the end of cooking. Seafood cooks quickly and is easily over cooked.

A note about the recipes: A recipe is a formula which is designed to have a successful end meaning it's a balanced formula which is successful and the end result provides you with something delicious to eat. Food is food. It is what it is and there are a finite number of foods so therefore a finite number of combinations.

These recipes are mine and I've chosen to share them with you. Yes, it's true, I do not eat meat but I still create recipes using meat because I not only have friends and family who are carnivores, I am also a professional Chef.

I've made every effort I can to ensure the nutritional information I've provided is accurate. My primary source for nutrition information has been caloriecount.com but I've also used others to double check those numbers.

I hope you enjoy reading and cooking with this book.

Soup:

I've intentionally chosen to include mostly vegetarian soup recipes in this book, the exception being two which contain seafood. One of the guidelines of the Mediterranean Diet is to eat at least one vegetarian meal a week. I think soup is an excellent choice to use as a food for transitioning into a plant based diet. As I was writing this I found the nutritional differences between the recipes which contain meat and those that do not both interesting and startling. If you read down through some of the calorie counts, you'll see what I meant. I think it's very interesting how easily we can eliminate fat and calories from our diet simply by reducing the meat consumption or eliminating it entirely.

There are as many different soup recipes as there are cooks with ingredients. These recipes are excellent as they're written but I also encourage you to use your creativity and make them your own. Don't have any cabbage for this vegetable soup recipe? That's OK. Substitutions are allowed. You could cut some Brussels sprouts in half and use those or even drain and rinse a can of beans and toss those in. Have fun and experiment!

With one exception, the seafood soup as noted, all of these recipes are based on a 6-qt. slow cooker.

A Note about Lentils:

Confused about the different types of lentils? Don't know what to do when a recipe says "lentils" but doesn't specify which type? Let's see if I can clear that up for you.

In very broad, general terms, there are three different types of lentils. These are the ones you'll most commonly find in stores:

Brown Lentils - This is by far the most common variety of lentil and for this reason is probably the one that you see at your local market. They're found in the aisle with the dried beans and are also available canned in some parts of the US. They can range in color from khaki-brown to dark black, and generally have a mild earthy flavor. They cook in as little as 20-30 minutes on the stove top and hold their shape very well. Common varieties are Spanish Brown, German Brown, or Indian Brown. Brown lentils are also very good in salads and for making veggie burgers.

When a recipe doesn't specify which type of lentil to use, it's a safe bet it's this one.

Green Lentils - These can be pale or mottled green-brown in color with a glossy exterior. They have a robust, somewhat peppery flavor. Green lentils generally take the longest to cook, upwards of 45 minutes, but they keep a firm texture even after cooking. This makes them ideal for salads and other side dishes. They're sold as Lentilles du Puy, Puy lentils, or French Green lentils.

Red Lentils - With colors ranging from gold to orange to actual red, these are the sweetest and nuttiest of the lentils. They're somewhere in the middle in terms of cooking time and are usually done in about 30 minutes. They have a tendency to completely fall apart when cooked through, so they're perfect for Indian dals and other curries, or for thickening soups. A few varieties are Red Chief and Crimson, and you'll often find them in Indian or Middle Eastern markets labeled as masoor (red lentils) or channa (yellow lentils).

There are also tiny, black lentils known as Beluga lentils. These have a rich and deeply earthy flavor.

I love lentils. They're fast cooking and don't require overnight soaking. They're easy to digest and have a deep, rich, earthy flavor.

Moroccan Red Lentil Soup

Total time: 1 hr. 10 min.

Prep time: 10 min.

Cook time: 60 min.

Serves: 6-7

Ingredients:

3 Tablespoons extra virgin olive oil

1 large onion, diced

1 celery stalk, diced

1 carrot, diced

4 cloves garlic, minced

2 teaspoon ground coriander

1 teaspoon ground cumin

1 teaspoon ground turmeric

1/2 teaspoon sweet paprika

1/4 teaspoon cinnamon

1 teaspoon kosher salt

1/2 teaspoon freshly ground black pepper

7 cups vegetable stock

1 (14.5 oz.) can crushed tomatoes

2 cups red lentils, picked over and washed

Juice1 lemon

Pinch of crushed red pepper flakes

4 Tablespoons fresh, flat leaf parsley, chopped

1 Tablespoon fresh cilantro, chopped

Directions:

In a large sauté pan heat olive oil over medium high heat until hot but not smoking.

Add the onions, carrots and celery and sauté about 3 or 4 minutes, or until tender.

Add the garlic, coriander, cumin, turmeric, paprika, cinnamon, salt and pepper and continue cooking for another 2-3 minutes, stirring continuously.

Add to the slow cooker along with the broth, tomatoes, and lentils. Stir well to combine and cover.

Set the slow cooker on low and cook for 6 – 8 hours.

When cooked, carefully remove half of the soup to a heatproof container and using an immersion blender, puree soup in small batches. Return the blended half of the soup to the slow cooker and mix well. If you prefer a chunky soup, simply skip this step.

Add lemon juice, red pepper flakes, parsley and cilantro during the last 30 minutes of cooking and cover tightly.

Serve hot with warm pita bread or bread of your choice. I enjoy a simply baked sweet potato as an accompaniment to this soup.

Garnish with extra parsley and cilantro or a small dollop of yogurt, if desired.

Nutrition Facts:

Serving Size 457 g

Amount Per Serving:

Calories: 333	Trans. Fat: 0.0g	Fiber: 22.6g
Calories from Fat: 73	Cholesterol: 0mg	Sugars: 6.6g
Total Fat: 8.1g	Sodium: 542mg	Protein: 18.7g
Sat. Fat: 1.1g	Carbs: 47.7g	

Lentil Spinach Soup

Total Time: 8 hrs. 20 mins.

Prep Time: 20 mins.

Cook Time: 8 hrs.

Servings: 8

Ingredients:

1 lb. lentils

1 quart vegetable broth

1 quart water

4 celery ribs, diced

4 carrots, peeled and diced

1 onion, diced

6 -8 garlic cloves, minced

1 1/2 cups vegetable stock

1 teaspoon dried oregano

1 bay leaf

3 sprigs fresh thyme

2 bay leaves

1 pinch cayenne pepper

Kosher salt, to taste

Freshly ground black pepper

10 oz. Baby Spinach, roughly chopped

Lemon wedges, for garnish, optional

Directions:

Combine all ingredients except spinach in crock pot. Cook on low heat for 8-10 hours, or until lentils have cooked and soup has thickened.

Stir in spinach and let sit, covered, a few minutes until spinach has completely wilted.

Nutritional Facts:

Serving Size: 1 (329 g)

Servings Per Recipe: 6

Amount Per Serving:

Calories: 197.2	Sodium: 635.1 mg
Calories from Fat: 14	Carbs: 40.3 g
Total Fat: 1.6 g	Fiber: 9.3 g
Sat. Fat: 0.2 g	Sugars: 7.5 g
Cholesterol: 0.0 mg	Protein: 7.7 g

Curried Lentil Soup

Total Time: 6 hrs. 20 mins.

Prep Time: 20 mins.

Cook Time: 6 hrs.

Servings: 6-8

Ingredients:

2 Tablespoons extra virgin olive oil

1 large onion, diced

2 garlic cloves, coarsely chopped

2 medium carrots, peeled and diced

1 cup portabella mushrooms, diced

2 Tablespoons tomato paste

1 cup dried lentils

6 cups vegetable stock

1 (14 1/2 ounce) can diced tomatoes with juice

2 Tablespoons curry powder

1 teaspoon dried oregano

1 teaspoon dried thyme

2 teaspoons freshly ground black pepper

Kosher salt, to taste

1/4 cup fresh cilantro, to garnish

Directions:

In a sauté pan over medium heat, heat the olive oil until hot but not smoking.

Add the onions and garlic and sauté for 3-5 minutes until they begin to brown.

Add the carrots and portabellas and sauté for another 3-5 minutes until the mushrooms begin to absorb the oil. Season with 1/2 teaspoon pepper and salt to taste.

Add the tomato paste and stir just to combine the vegetables.

In the bottom of your crock pot, add the curry powder, oregano, thyme and remaining pepper. Add the sautéed vegetables and lentils and mix well.

Pour in the diced tomatoes and stock. Stir to combine and add salt to taste.

Cook in a crock pot on high heat for 6 hours.

Garnish with cilantro and serve.

Nutritional Facts:

Serving Size: 1 (131 g)

Servings Per Recipe: 6

Amount Per Serving:

Calories: 208.9	Sodium: 210.6 mg
Calories from Fat: 48	Carbs: 32.0 g
Total Fat: 5.4 g	Fiber: 13.1 g
Sat. Fat: 0.7 g	Sugars: 6.1 g
Cholesterol: 0.0 mg	Protein: 10.2 g

The Easiest Lentil Soup I Know

Total Time: 6 hrs. 5 mins.

Prep Time: 5 mins.

Cook Time: 6 hrs.

Servings: 4

This is so ridiculously easy I didn't include it in the recipe count for this book because it's barely a recipe at all.

Here's what you do:

Take a pound of lentils; pick them over to remove seeds and any stones. Wash them well. Dump them in the slow cooker. Throw in a package of frozen, chopped spinach (Nope. No need to wait for it to thaw.), 1 (16 oz.) jar of salsa, 2 bay leaves and 6 cups of water or stock. Add some kosher salt and freshly ground black pepper, put the lid on, fire the slow cooker up and let it cook on Low for about 6 hours. It's soup!

You can add anything you like to this. Try carrots, celery, onion, garlic, mushrooms, corn or sweet potatoes. Toss in a handful of barley.

Garnish it with sour cream, yogurt, cream cheese, cheese, diced tomatoes, scallions, avocado, olives, salsa verde, bacon bits, roasted chilies, cilantro, lemon wedges, drizzle some extra virgin olive oil over the top, do whatever suits your fancy!

Nutrition Facts

Serving Size 199 g

Amount Per Serving:

Calories: 298	Carbs: 51.9g
Calories from Fat: 10	Fiber: 25.3g
Total Fat: 1.1g	Sugars: 4.0g
Cholesterol: 0mg	Protein: 22.0g
Sodium; 786mg	

Basque Black Bean Soup

Total Time: 6 hrs.

Prep Time: 1 hrs.

Cook Time: 5 hrs.

Servings: 10

The age of your beans can cause great variation in cooking time. As beans age, they lose moisture and take longer to cook. When you buy dry beans you have no way of knowing their age. I find this to be especially true with black beans.

Ingredients:

1 lb. dried black beans

1 1/2 quarts vegetable stock

1 carrot, chopped

1 stalk celery, chopped

1 large red onion, chopped

6 cloves garlic, crushed

2 green bell peppers, chopped

2 jalapeno peppers, chopped

1/4 cup lentils

1 (28 ounce) can diced tomatoes

2 Tablespoons chili powder

2 teaspoons ground cumin

1/2 teaspoon dried oregano

1/2 teaspoon ground black pepper

3 Tablespoons red wine vinegar

1 Tablespoon kosher salt

Lime wedges

Cilantro

Avocado chunks

Directions:

Pick over and wash beans.

Place beans in a bowl and cover with a generous amount of water. Cover and let sit overnight.

Next Day:

Drain beans, transfer to slow cooker and combine beans with 1 1/2 quarts vegetable stock.

Cover and cook for 3-7 hours on high, depending on how hot your slow cooker gets.

Add carrot, celery, onion, garlic, bell pepper, jalapeno, lentils and tomatoes.

Season with chili powder, cumin, oregano, black pepper, red wine vinegar and salt.

Cook on low, 2 to 3 hours.

Carefully puree half the soup with an immersion blender and pour back into slow cooker. Heat through before serving.

Serve with lime wedges, avocado chunks, and cilantro.

Nutrition Facts:

Serving Size 347 g

Amount Per Serving:

Calories:212	Sodium:170mg
Calories from Fat:10	Carbs:39.1g
Total Fat: 1.1g	Fiber:11.2g
Trans Fat:0.0g	Sugars:6.1g
Cholesterol: 0mg	Protein:12.9g

Vegetable Soup

Total Time: 4 hrs. 30 mins.

Prep Time: 30 mins.

Cook Time: 4 hrs.

Servings: 12

Ingredients:

1 large onion, chopped

4 cloves garlic, minced

2 Tablespoons extra virgin olive oil, divided

2 large carrots, peeled and diced

2 stalks celery, diced

1 medium turnip, peeled and diced

2 cups green beans, cut in 1-inch pieces

1/4 head cabbage, chopped

1/2 teaspoon thyme

2 (14 oz.) cans diced tomatoes, undrained

8 cups chicken or vegetable stock

Kosher salt, to taste

Freshly ground black pepper

2 small potatoes, peeled and diced

Directions:

In a large soup pot, heat 1 Tablespoon olive oil over medium high heat until hot but not smoking.

Add onion and cook for 3 or 4 minutes. Do not brown.

Add garlic and sauté for 1 minute.

Add the remaining tablespoon of olive oil to the pan along with all the vegetables except potatoes and canned tomatoes and sauté for 2 minutes.

Add thyme, salt and pepper to vegetables.

Transfer vegetables to the slow cooker, adding tomatoes, potatoes and broth.

Cook on low 7-9 hours or high 4-6 hours.

Just before serving, gently mash some of the potato chunks against the side of the slow cooker to thicken the soup, and stir well to combine.

This is a great base soup for variations too! Try one of these or create your own delectable delights!

It's easy to make the basic soup recipe and then dress up smaller portions for variety.

Autumn Vegetable Soup: **Add some diced sweet potatoes and a generous handful of baby spinach. Season with a dash of nutmeg.**

Harvest Vegetable Soup: **Add some diced butternut or acorn squash, a spoonful of cooked brown rice, a sprinkling of cinnamon and some chopped parsley.**

Tuscan Vegetable Soup: **Drain and rinse canned cannellini or other white beans and add them along with a pinch of Italian seasoning and some chopped kale. Cook until the kale is tender.**

Tex- Mex Soup: **Drain and rinse canned black beans and add them along with a pinch of cumin and some chopped cilantro. Top with tortilla chips and avocado slices.**

Nutritional Facts:

Serving Size: 1 (292 g)

Servings Per Recipe: 12

Amount Per Serving:

Calories: 97.7	Sodium 400.8 mg
Calories from Fat: 28	Carbs: 13.6 g
Total Fat: 3.2 g	Fiber: 3.1 g
Sat. Fat: 0.5 g	Sugars: 5.0 g
Cholesterol: 0.0 mg	Protein: 4.5 g

Borscht

Total Time: 9 hrs. 20 mins.

Prep Time: 20 mins.

Cook Time: 9 hrs.

Servings: 4

I love everything about beets! To me they're the essence of just about everything that's good about the earth. They're the color of a wonderful day and they have a sweet, earthy flavor that speaks of the soil they were grown in. If you've never tried beets, this is a great place to start!

Ingredients:

2 bunches red beets

3/4 lb. russet potato, peeled and cut in half

1 large yellow onion, peeled and into quarters

2 carrots, peeled and cut into large chunks

32 ozs. vegetable broth

1 Tablespoon tomato paste

1 teaspoon whole caraway seed

Kosher salt, to taste

3 cups finely shredded green cabbage (about 1/4 small head)

1/4 cup fresh dill, chopped, plus

3 Tablespoons fresh dill, chopped

1 Tablespoon red wine vinegar, to taste

1-2 Tablespoons lemon juice, or to taste

Choose one or all of the following:

Low fat sour cream or yogurt, for garnish

Lemon wedges, for garnish

Fresh dill, snipped, for garnish

Fresh tomatoes, diced, for garnish

Beets, cut in small dice, for garnish

Directions:

Remove tops from beets and set aside for another use. Cut beets in half if larger than 2 inches in diameter.

Place beets, potato, onion, broth, caraway seed and tomato paste in slow cooker and cook on high heat for 4 hours or low heat for 8 hours.

Fish out the beets, place them on a plate and allow them to cool until cool enough to handle. Slip off the beet skins using your fingers.

Carefully process soup in batches in a blender until smooth and return to slow cooker. Do not fill blender canister more than half full, and make sure that the top is securely attached.

45 minutes before you are ready to serve, bury the cabbage in the pureed soup. Increase you temperature setting to high and cook, covered.

Add 1/4 cup dill, vinegar and lemon juice and season to taste with salt.

In a separate bowl, mix remainder of dill with sour cream or yogurt. Serve with a dollop of the sour cream in each bowl of soup and with lemon wedges.

Alternately, if you don't own a blender or food processor or prefer a chunky soup, peel the beets and dice in 1/4" dice before cooking.

Borscht is delicious served either hot or cold.

Nutrition Facts:

Serving Size 781 g

Amount Per Serving:

Calories: 302	Sat. Fat: 0.6g	Sodium:1031mg	Sugars:33.3g
Calories from Fat: 21	Trans Fat:0.0g	Carbs: 60.7g	Protein:14.1g
Total Fat: 2.3g	Cholesterol:0mg	Fiber:12.0g	

Mushroom - Barley Soup

Total Time: 6 hrs. 30 mins.

Prep Time: 15 mins.

Cook Time: 6 hrs. 45 mins.

Servings: 4-6

Ingredients:

1 oz. dried mushrooms

1 Tablespoon extra virgin olive oil

1 onion, chopped

1 carrot, chopped

1 celery rib, chopped

1 cup pearled barley

8 oz. mushrooms, sliced

6 cups vegetable broth

1 teaspoon dried thyme

1 Tablespoon tamari

Kosher salt, to taste

Freshly ground black pepper

!/4 cup dry Sherry

2 Tablespoons chives, minced

Directions:

Place the dried mushrooms in a heatproof measuring cup and cover with hot water. Let stand, covered, until softened. Drain, reserving 1/2 cup of the liquid. Slice mushrooms. Set aside.

In a small skillet heat olive oil over medium heat until hot but not smoking. Add onion, carrot and celery and cook until softened, about 5 minutes.

Transfer vegetables to crock pot and add barley, both kinds of mushrooms, broth, and reserved mushroom soaking liquid, thyme, tamari, salt and pepper. Cover and cook on low for 6 hours.

30 minutes before serving, add sherry, stir well, replace lid and continue to cook.

Serve garnished with chives.

Nutritional Facts:

Serving Size: 1 (114 g)

Servings Per Recipe: 4

Amount Per Serving:

Calories: 260.3	Sodium: 28.0 mg
Calories from Fat: 39	Carbs: 51.0 g
Total Fat: 4.3 g	Fiber: 10.3 g
Sat. Fat: 0.6 g	Sugars: 5.0 g
Cholesterol: 0.0 mg	Protein: 7.9 g

Barley Vegetable Soup

Total Time: 6 hrs. 20 mins.

Prep Time: 20 mins.

Cook Time: 6 hrs.

Servings: 6

Ingredients:

6 cups vegetable broth

2 carrots, chopped

2 large onions, chopped

3 celery ribs, chopped

2 cloves garlic, minced

1 small zucchini, cubed

1 handful fresh kale, chopped

1/2 cup pearled barley

1 (14 1/2 ounce) can chickpeas or white beans, rinsed and drained

1 Tablespoon fresh parsley, minced

1/2 teaspoon dried thyme

1 teaspoon dried oregano

1 teaspoon marjoram

1 (28 oz.) can crushed Italian tomatoes

1 teaspoon kosher salt

1/4 teaspoon freshly ground black pepper

Pesto, for garnish (recipe follows)

Extra Virgin olive oil, for drizzling

Directions:

Combine all ingredients except cheese in slow cooker.

Cover.

Cook on Low 6-8 hours, or until vegetables are tender.

Serve topped with a spoonful of pesto and a drizzle of extra virgin olive oil.

Nutritional Facts:

Serving Size: 1 (329 g)

Servings Per Recipe: 6

Amount Per Serving:

Calories: 197.2	Sodium: 635.1 mg
Calories from Fat: 14	Carbs: 40.3 g
Total Fat: 1.6 g	Fiber: 9.3 g
Sat. Fat: 0.2 g	Sugars: 7.5 g
Cholesterol: 0.0 mg	Protein: 7.7 g

Tuscan Bean and Kale Soup

Total Time: 6 hrs. 15 mins.

Prep Time: 15 mins.

Cook Time: 6 hrs.

Servings: 10

Ingredients:

3 Tablespoons extra virgin olive oil

1 onion, chopped

3 carrots, chopped

2 stalks celery, with leaves, chopped

1 clove garlic, chopped

1/2 teaspoon dried rosemary

1/2 teaspoon dried thyme

1/4 teaspoon crushed red pepper flakes

1 lb. dried white beans

Kosher salt and freshly ground black pepper, to taste

8 cups vegetable stock

8 oz. kale, stems removed, leaves torn into small pieces

4 oz. Parmesan cheese, for garnish

Extra virgin olive oil, for drizzling

1 lemon for garnish

Directions:

The night before: Pick over the beans removing any dirt and debris, wash well, place in a bowl and cover with a generous amount of water. Allow to sit overnight.

Next morning: drain and place beans in slow cooker.

Heat 3 Tbsp. olive oil in a sauté pan until hot but not smoking, add onion, carrots, and celery and cook until soft.

Add the vegetables to the slow cooker along with the seasonings and stock.

Cook on high for 4 hours or on low for 8 hours.

Check beans near end of cooking time and add additional stock as needed.

1 hour before serving, add the kale. This will seem like an enormous amount of kale but it does cook down. You might need to add it in 2 batches.

Garnish with lemon wedges, and Parmesan cheese. Drizzle with extra virgin olive oil.

Nutritional Facts:

Serving Size: 1 (297 g)

Servings Per Recipe: 10

Amount Per Serving:

Calories: 254.1	Sodium: 398.1 mg
Calories from Fat: 71	Carbs: 31.7 g
Total Fat: 7.9 g	Fiber: 7.9 g
Sat. Fat: 2.6 g	Sugars: 2.8 g
Cholesterol :10.1 mg	Protein: 15.6 g

Golden Mushroom Soup

Total Time: 6 hrs. 20 mins.

Prep Time: 20 mins.

Cook Time: 6 hrs.

Servings: 4

Yield: 6 cups

Ingredients:

2 Tablespoons extra virgin olive oil

2 onions, finely chopped

4 scallions, minced

2 cloves garlic, finely chopped

2 carrots, finely chopped

4 cups oyster mushrooms, sliced

3 cups button mushrooms, sliced

2 cups portabella caps, diced

1 bay leaf

1/2 teaspoon thyme

1/4 teaspoon smoked paprika

1/4 teaspoon freshly ground black pepper

Kosher salt, to taste

5 cups vegetable stock

1 potato, peeled and thinly sliced

2 Tablespoons red wine

1 Tablespoon tamari

Directions:

In large sauté pan over medium, heat olive oil until hot but not smoking, add onions, scallions, and carrots and cook until softened, about 5 minutes.

Stir in garlic, mushrooms, thyme, paprika and pepper; cook stirring often until no liquid remains, about 10 minutes.

Scrape into slow cooker.

Add 1 cup broth to skillet and bring to a boil, scraping up any browned bits that are stuck to the pan.

Scrape into slow cooker along with remaining broth and potato. Stir to combine.

Cover and cook on low until vegetables are tender and liquid is slightly thickened, about 6 hours.

Stir in cooking wine and tamari.

Excellent served with a salad containing Gorgonzola cheese and a crusty loaf of French bread.

Nutritional Facts:

Serving Size: 1 (512 g)

Servings Per Recipe: 4

Amount Per Serving:

Calories: 205.1	Sodium: 983.1 mg
Calories from Fat: 79	Carbs: 21.4 g
Total Fat: 8.8 g	Fiber: 3.4 g
Sat. Fat: 1.4 g	Sugars: 5.9 g
Cholesterol: 0.0 mg	Protein: 9.6 g

Vegetarian Split Pea Soup

Total Time: 4 hrs. 10 mins.

Prep Time: 10 mins.

Cook Time: 4 hrs.

Servings: 6-8

Season this soup with toasted sesame seed oil and you'll never miss the ham!

Ingredients:

3 cups dried split peas

7 cups water (may need more) or 7 cups vegetable stock (may need more)

1 bay leaf

1 teaspoon kosher salt

1 teaspoon dry mustard

2 cups onions, minced

4 medium cloves garlic, minced

3 stalks celery, minced

2 medium carrots, sliced

Freshly ground black pepper

2 - 4 tablespoons tamari

Sesame oil, as garnish

Fresh ripe Tomato, diced, as garnish

Fresh parsley, minced, as garnish

Additional tamari, as garnish

Directions:

Pick over peas, removing any seeds or debris. Wash thoroughly under cold water. Place in slow cooker.

Layer ingredients in slow cooker in order listed above. Do not stir.

Cover and cook until peas are soft High: 4-5 hours or Low: 8-10 hours

Remove bay leaf before serving.

Garnish before serving.

Adding toasted sesame oil to this soup gives it a completely different flavor you won't want to miss!

Nutritional Facts:

Serving Size: 1 (386 g)

Servings Per Recipe: 6

Amount Per Serving:

Calories: 403.1	Sodium: 833.5 mg
Calories from Fat: 12	Carbs: 74.4 g
Total Fat: 1.4 g	Fiber: 27.7
Sat. Fat: 0.2 g	Sugars: 12.1 g
Cholesterol: 0.0 mg	Protein: 26.0 g

Fasolatha (Greek Bean Soup)

Total Time: 7-9 hrs. 5 mins. Plus additional time to soak beans overnight.

Prep Time: 5 mins

Cook Time: 7 -9 hrs.

Servings: 7

The Fasolatha (bean soup) Festival originated in Florina, Macedonia, Greece, and is now a major cultural event in many Greek communities.

Serve this wonderful soup with a traditional Greek Salad and some toasted Pita triangles.

Traditionally, most Fasolatha recipes call for as much as a cup or more of good quality olive oil to be cooked in the soup. I prefer to reduce the amount of oil in the soup to save some fat calories and add additional extra virgin olive oil to my bowl when serving because I really enjoy the flavor of good quality olive oil in its raw state, especially in this soup.

Ingredients:

1 lb. navy beans (or any other small dried white bean)

3 carrots, peeled and sliced

1 onion, peeled and chopped

3 stalks celery, chopped (leaves included)

1 cup tomato sauce

6 cups chicken or vegetable stock

1/4 cup good quality extra virgin olive oil

Kosher salt, to taste

Freshly ground black pepper

Lemon wedges for garnish

Good quality extra virgin olive oil for drizzling

Directions:

Soak the beans in water over night.

Strain the water and place the beans in the slow cooker.

Add remaining ingredients, cover and cook on low for 7 – 9 hours.

Cooking times will vary based on the age of your beans. Older beans take longer to cook.

Serve in bowls with lemon wedges and drizzle with olive oil.

Nutritional Facts:

Serving Size: 1 (189 g)

Servings Per Recipe: 7

Amount Per Serving:

Calories: 391.6	Sodium: 369.9 mg
Calories from Fat: 282	Carbs: 23.2 g
Total Fat: 31.4 g	Fiber: 8.6 g
Sat. Fat: 4.3 g	Sugars: 3.9 g
Cholesterol: 0.0 mg	Protein: 6.3 g

Spinach-Vegetable Soup

Total Time: 5 hrs. 10 mins.

Prep Time: 10 mins.

Cook Time: 5 hrs.

Servings: 10

Ingredients:

1 lb. baby spinach

2 medium carrots, chopped

2 medium celery ribs, chopped

1 large onion, chopped

2 cloves garlic, minced

4 cups vegetable broth

1 (28 oz.) can diced tomatoes

2 bay leaves

1 Tablespoon dried basil

1 teaspoon dried oregano

1/2 teaspoon crushed red pepper flakes

Kosher salt and freshly ground black pepper, to taste

Directions:

Place all ingredients in a slow cooker.

Cover and cook on high for 5 hours.

Remove bay leaves, stir and serve.

Pass hot sauce at the table, if desired.

Nutritional Facts:

Serving Size: 1 (143 g)

Servings Per Recipe: 10

Amount Per Serving:

Calories: 34.5	Sodium: 42.0 mg
Calories from Fat: 3	Carbs: 7.2 g
Total Fat: 0.3 g	Fiber: 2.4 g
Sat. Fat: 0.0 g	Sugars: 3.5 g
Cholesterol: 0.0 mg	Protein: 1.9 g

Seafood Stew

Total Time: 5 hrs.

Prep Time: 30 mins.

Cook Time: 4 hrs. 30 mins.

Servings: 6-8

Ingredients:

1 Tablespoon extra virgin olive oil

2 onions, diced

4 stalks celery, chopped

4 cloves garlic, minced

1 teaspoon dried oregano

1/2 teaspoon black peppercorns, cracked

1 Tablespoon tomato paste

1 Tablespoon flour

3 cups vegetable or chicken stock

1 (10 oz.) can tomatoes and green chilies

1 -2 cups tomato juice

1 lb. chicken breast, cut into bite size pieces

8 oz. shrimp, thawed

5 oz. clams

2 red bell peppers, chopped

1 jalapeno pepper, chopped

1/4 cup parsley, chopped

1 teaspoon chili powder

1 pinch cayenne pepper

8 oz. scallops, halved

1 Tablespoon butter

Hot pepper sauce

Directions:

In a large sauté pan, heat the olive oil over medium heat until hot but not smoking.

Add onions and celery and cook, stirring, until tender, about 5 minutes

Add garlic, oregano, peppercorns, cook, stirring, for one minute.

Stir in tomato paste and flour, cook for one minute.

Add broth, tomatoes and tomato juice and bring to a boil. Continue to cook for about 3-5 minutes. Transfer mixture to slow cooker.

Add chicken and stir to combine. Cover, cook on Low for 6 hours or High for 3 hours.

Add shrimp, clams, peppers, and parsley. Stir to combine, cover and cook on High for 30 minutes.

Meanwhile, combine chili powder and cayenne in a zip top bag. Add scallops and shake well to coat.

In a sauté pan over medium heat, melt butter. Remove scallops from bag, shaking off excess coating, add scallops to butter and cook. Cook scallops for 3-5 minutes, stirring occasionally, until scallops are opaque.

Add scallops to slow cooker, stir gently so scallops don't break up.

Pass hot sauce at the table, if desired.

Nutritional Facts:

Serving Size: 1 (288 g)

Servings Per Recipe: 6

Amount Per Serving:

Calories: 295.5	Sodium: 921.1 mg
Calories from Fat: 110	Carbs: 15.0 g
Total Fat: 12.3 g	Fiber: 2.6 g
Sat. Fat: 3.7 g	Sugars: 4.9 g
Cholesterol: 117.2 mg	Protein: 31.1 g

Italian Seafood and Fennel Stew

Total Time: 2 hrs. 50 mins.

Prep Time: 20 mins.

Cook Time: 2 hrs. 30 mins.

Servings: 6-10

YUM! This is a fun dish for a leisurely meal with family and friends. Serve in wide, flat soup bowls with plenty of crusty bread.

This is an expensive dish to make so don't skimp on the price of tomatoes. You won't regret it. San Marzano tomatoes will make this dish exceptional. I think all other canned tomatoes pale by comparison.

Ingredients:

4 cups seafood or chicken stock

2 cups dry white wine

1/2 cup extra virgin olive oil

1 medium onion, chopped

6 cloves garlic, sliced thin

1/2 cup Italian parsley, minced

2 cups fresh fennel, cut in small julienne

1 cup carrot, cut in small julienne

1 cup celery, cut in small julienne

2 lbs. large sea scallops

2 lbs. mussels, beards removed and scrubbed well

1 lb. large shrimp, peeled and deveined, tails left on

1 (28 ounce) can San Marzano tomatoes, undrained

2 Tablespoons fresh lemon

1/2 cup Italian parsley, chopped fine

Kosher salt, to taste

Freshly ground black pepper

Additional parsley for garnish

Crusty French bread for mopping up the juices

Directions:

In a 8.5 quart slow cooker, combine seafood stock, wine, and olive oil.

Add onion, parsley, and garlic to the liquid, cover, and cook on high for one hour.

Add the carrots, fennel, and celery, cover and cook 30-45 minutes on high.

Add the seafood to the slow cooker and layer in this order: mussels, sea scallops, and shrimp.

"Smoosh" the tomatoes up with your fingers so they're broken into small pieces and add to the slow cooker along with the juice from the tomatoes, lemon juice, salt, and pepper.

Cover and cook on High for 30-45 more minutes.

Ladle into serving bowls and garnish with parsley..

Serve with crusty bread or garlic bread and a big green salad.

Nutritional Facts:

Serving Size: 1 (414 g)

Servings Per Recipe: 6

Amount Per Serving:

Calories: 667.1	Sodium: 1173.5 mg
Calories from Fat: 240	Carbs: 27.1 g
Total Fat: 26.6 g	Fiber: 4.0 g
Sat. Fat: 5.0 g	Sugars: 6.4 g
Cholesterol: 214.8 mg	Protein: 64.2 g

Beans:

White Beans with Sun-Dried Tomatoes
Total Time: 5 hrs. 10 mins.

Prep Time: 10 mins.

Cook Time: 5 hrs.

Servings: 6

This is my personal go to bean recipe. It's a very easy recipe to just throw together and have in the fridge or freezer and I love beans, all beans. I eat about 4 pounds of beans a month cooked in this way because they're good hot or cold and can be combined with so many other foods. They're better cooked a day in advance and refrigerated overnight. You can add several handfuls of greens such as kale to this recipe once it is almost cooked and serve it over rice. They also go very well in a salad when combined with oil packed tuna or shrimp and roasted red peppers. They're delicious mashed with some extra virgin olive oil, fresh rosemary and oil cured Italian olives to make a spread or dip. The dried tomatoes add a subtle smokiness to this recipe you might not expect.

Since I cook more by eye than measurement, I probably use more crushed red pepper flakes than this recipe states. I like my food spicy!

Ingredients:

1 lb. dried great northern beans or other small white beans

6 cloves garlic, finely chopped

6 cups vegetable stock

2 Tablespoons extra virgin olive oil

3/4 cup sun-dried tomato packed in oil, finely chopped

2 bay leaves

1 teaspoon dried rosemary, crushed

1/2 teaspoon dried thyme leaves

1 teaspoon kosher salt

1/4 teaspoon freshly ground pepper

1/4 teaspoon crushed red pepper

Parmesan Cheese, for garnish

Extra virgin olive oil for drizzling

Directions:

Pick over beans removing any seeds or debris. Place in a large bowl and cover with a generous amount of cold water. Refrigerate overnight.

Next morning: Drain beans and place in slow cooker with all other ingredients.

Cover and cook on High 4 to 5 hours or until beans are tender.

Nutritional Facts:

Serving Size: 1 (407 g)

Servings Per Recipe: 5

Amount Per Serving:

Calories: 360.0	Cholesterol: 0.0 mg
Calories from Fat: 42	Carbs: 61.8 g
Total Fat: 4.7 g	Fiber: 19.8 g
Sat. Fat 0.8 g	Sugars: 2.0 g
Sodium: 637.5 mg	Protein: 20.9 g

White Beans with Pesto

Total Time: 6 hrs. 10 mins.

Prep Time: 10 mins.

Cook Time: 6 hrs.

Servings: 6-8

This is especially good in the summer when the garden is full of fresh herbs and vegetables. There's nothing on this planet quite as delicious as a home grown heirloom tomato which has spent its day being warmed by the sun!

Ingredients:

2 Tablespoons extra virgin olive oil

2 large sweet onions, roughly chopped

2 red bell peppers, seeded and diced

4 large ripe tomatoes, peeled, seeded, and chopped or 1 (14 1/2 ounce) can diced tomatoes

1/2 cup sun dried tomatoes, chopped

6 cups cooked cannellini beans or 6 cups cooked white kidney beans, drained and rinsed, if canned.

3 cups vegetable broth

Kosher salt, to taste

Freshly ground black pepper

1/2 cup basil pesto (recipe follows)

Directions:

Heat the oil in a medium size sauté pan over medium heat until hot but not smoking. Add onion, cover, and cook until softened, about 5 minutes.

Transfer the onion to a slow cooker. Add the bell pepper both kinds of tomatoes, beans, and stock; season with salt and pepper, cover, and cook on low for 6-8 hours.

Just before serving, stir in the pesto.

Serve over small tubular pasta or pasta shells with a side of grilled Italian bread. I like to use Ditalini.

Nutritional Facts

Serving Size: 1 (402 g)

Servings Per Recipe: 6-8

Amount Per Serving:

Calories: 273.9	Sodium: 88.3 mg
Calories from Fat: 39	Carbs: 46.1 g
Total Fat: 4.3 g	Fiber: 11.7 g
Sat. Fat: 0.6 g	Sugars: 8.1 g
Cholesterol: 0.0 mg	Protein: 15.4 g

Basil Pesto

Prep time: 10 minutes

Yield: Makes 1 cup.

Ingredients:

2 cups fresh basil leaves, packed

1/2 cup freshly grated Parmesan-Reggiano, Romano or Parmesan cheese

1/2 cup extra virgin olive oil

1/3 cup pine nuts or walnuts

3 medium cloves garlic, minced

Salt and freshly ground black pepper to taste

Directions:

Wash basil well. Dry with paper towels.

Place basil and pine nuts in the work bowl of food processor and pulse a few times. (If you're using walnut halves instead of pine nuts, pulse them a few times before adding the basil.) Add the garlic and cheese and pulse a few times more.

Slowly drizzle the olive oil in a constant stream down the feed tube with the food processor on. Stop to scrape down the sides of the food processor with a rubber spatula. Add a pinch of salt and freshly ground black pepper to taste.

Nutrition Facts

Serving Size 41 g

Amount Per Serving

Calories:216	Cholesterol:3mg
Calories from Fat:207	Sodium:44mg
Total Fat:23.0g	Total Carbs:2.3g
Sat. Fat:3.4g	Protein:3.0g

White Bean and Cabbage Soup

Total Time: 7 hrs. 10 mins.

Prep Time: 10 mins.

Cook Time: 7 hrs.

Servings: 4-6

Ingredients:

1 large onion, chopped

3 celery ribs, chopped

3 cloves garlic, minced

1/2 head cabbage, chopped

4 carrots, sliced

1 lb. potato, diced

1/3 cup pearl barley

1 bay leaf

1 teaspoon thyme

1/2 teaspoon caraway seed

1/2 teaspoon rosemary

1/2 teaspoon freshly ground black pepper

6-8 cups vegetable stock

28 oz. (2-14 oz. cans) great northern beans or other small white beans

1 (14 oz.) can diced tomatoes

1 Tablespoon chopped parsley

Kosher salt, to taste

Sour Cream, garnish

Snipped chives, garnish

Directions:

Place the onions, garlic, celery, cabbage, potatoes, seasonings, and barley in the slow cooker.

Add enough vegetable stock to just cover the vegetables, beginning with 6 cups and adding more as needed.

Cover and cook on low heat for 7 hours.

Add beans, tomatoes, parsley, and salt to taste. Check seasonings and add more herbs if necessary. Cover and cook for 1 hour.

Serve topped with sour cream and snipped chives.

Nutritional Facts:

Serving Size: 1 (420 g)

Servings Per Recipe: 4

Amount Per Serving:

Calories: 432.2	Sodium: 315.4 mg
Calories from Fat: 14	Carb: 89.7 g
Total Fat: 1.5 g	Fiber: 22.9 g
Sat. Fat: 0.3 g	Sugars: 13.7 g
Cholesterol: 0.0 mg	Protein: 20.6 g

White Beans Squash Kale and Olive Stew

Total Time: 10 hrs. 15 mins.

Prep Time: 15 mins.

Cook Time: 10 hrs.

Servings: 6

Ingredients:

1/4 cup extra virgin olive oil

1 large onion, chopped

6 cloves garlic, minced

1/4 teaspoon crushed red pepper flakes

2 Tablespoon dried rubbed sage

1 (3 lb.) butternut squash, peeled, seeded and cut into 1 inch cubes

1 red bell pepper, seeded and cut into 3/4" squares

32oz. vegetable stock

1/2 bunch kale, thick stems removed and leaves cut crosswise into 2 inch strips

2 (15 oz.) cans cannellini beans, rinsed and drained

1/4 cup Kalamata olive, pitted and halved

Kosher salt, to taste

Freshly ground black pepper

Freshly grated Romano cheese, as garnish

Extra virgin olive oil for drizzling at the table

Directions:

In a large sauté pan, heat 1/4 cup olive oil until hot but not smoking. Add onions and sauté until translucent. Add garlic, crushed red pepper flakes, and sage, remove from heat, and set aside.

Combine all ingredients in the slow cooker except the cheese and extra virgin for drizzling.

Cook on low for 8 to 10 hours or on high for 5 to 6 hours.

Transfer to large, shallow serving bowl and sprinkle generously with grated cheese and drizzle with olive oil.

Nutritional Facts:

Serving Size: 1 (623 g)

Servings Per Recipe: 6

Amount Per Serving:

Calories: 544	Carbs 100.5g
Total Calories From Fat: 20	Fiber 39.0g
Total Fat 2.2g	Sugars 7.8g
Cholesterol 0mg	Protein 35.5g
Sodium: 163mg	

Seafood:

The slow cooker is great for seafood. The only down side is that you can't put it in in the morning, and come home to a fish dinner at night. However, most fish and seafood cooks quickly, so you can cook the base all day, and pop the seafood in when you get home at the end of the day, and it will be ready for dinner.

Seafood is so healthy and filled with nutrients that may help fight some cancers, heart disease, improve cognitive functions, and aid in eye health. It may even help you look younger too.

Greek Shrimp and Feta Cheese
Total Time: 6-8 hrs. 25mins.

Prep Time: 10 mins.

Cook Time: 10 hrs.

Servings: 8

Ingredients:

2 Tablespoons extra virgin olive oil

1 medium onion, chopped

1 clove garlic, minced

1(28 oz.) canned San Marzano tomatoes

1 (12 oz.) can tomato paste

1/4 cup dry white wine

2 tablespoons parsley, chopped

1 teaspoon dried oregano

1/4 teaspoon freshly ground black pepper

1 1/2 pound medium shrimp, peeled and deveined

2 oz. feta cheese, crumbled

Directions

In a medium sauté pan heat olive oil until hot but not smoking. Add onion and cook about 4-5 minutes or until onions are soft. Add garlic and cook for 1 minute, do not brown.

Combine all ingredients except shrimp and feta in crockpot.

Cover; cook on Low for 6-8 hours. Turn heat to High; add shrimp, cook about 15 minutes or until just pink. Stir in feta cheese and serve.

Nutritional Facts:

Serving Size: 1 (623 g)

Servings Per Recipe: 8

Amount Per Serving:

Calories 204	Potassium:818mg
Total Fat: 7g	Total Carbs: 15g
Sat. Fat: 2g	Fiber: 3g
Cholesterol: 136mg	Protein:21g
Sodium: 689mg	

Atum Basco com Batatas e Pimentões Vermelho
Basque Tuna with Potatoes and Peppers

Total Time: 2-4 hrs. 25 mins.

Prep Time: 25 mins.

Cook Time: 2-4 hrs.

Servings: 6.

Ingredients:

2 Tablespoons extra virgin olive oil

2 Tablespoons smoked paprika, or more to taste

1 teaspoon kosher salt

1-1/2 lbs. fresh tuna, cut into 1-1/2 inch chunks

1 large sweet onion, cut into wedges

6 large cloves garlic, chopped

1 teaspoon freshly ground black pepper

1/2 cup dry white wine

2 cups San Marzano tomatoes, undrained

3 potatoes, unpeeled and cut in chunks

1 cup chicken stock

1 green bell pepper, cut into 3/4" pieces

1 red bell pepper, cut into 3/4" pieces

1/4 cup green olives, pitted

1/4 cup Kalamata olives, pitted

1 Tablespoon cornstarch

Lemon wedges, for garnish

Directions

In a bowl, combine olive oil, smoked paprika, salt and tuna chunks. Toss until fish is well coated. Cover and refrigerate.

"Smoosh" the tomatoes up with your fingers and add to the slow cooker along with the onion, garlic, black pepper, wine, diced tomatoes, potatoes and chicken stock. Cook on High for 2 hours or on Low for 4 hours.

Add the bell peppers and olives, and cook on High for 1 hour.

Add the tuna chunks and the marinade. Cover and cook on High for 30 minutes.

Transfer the tuna and vegetables to a serving bowl and cover to keep warm.

Pour the liquid from the slow cooker into a small saucepan, and bring to a boil.

Place cornstarch in a small dish or measuring cup and add 2 tablespoons of cold water. Pour into the liquid in the sauce pan in a small stream, stirring continuously. When it has thickened slightly, pour over the fish and vegetables.

Garnish with lemon wedges.

Serve hot, over polenta, couscous or brown rice with a green salad and a crusty loaf of bread.

This may be prepared up to 3 days in advance.

Nutrition Facts:

Serving Size 372 g

Amount Per Serving

Calories; 317	Sodium: 630mg
Calories from Fat: 107	Carbs:25.9g
Total Fat:11.9g	Fiber: 4.8g
Sat. Fat: 2.1g	Sugars: 5.5g
Cholesterol: 23mg	Protein: 23.2g

Basic Polenta

Total Time: 40 mins

Prep Time: 5 mins

Cook Time: 35 mins

Servings: 4-6

This is a technique more than it is a recipe. It is not cooked in a slow cooker but rather in a pot on top of the stove. I felt I should include it in this book because not only is it delicious, it also makes a great accompaniment for many of these recipes.

Somewhere, polenta picked up a reputation for being hard to make. I can tell you that it is not that fussy and once you've made it once or twice, you'll be able to whip up a pot of creamy polenta in about 30 minutes. Polenta makes a luscious bed for anything from quickly sautéed mushrooms to a hearty slow-simmered ragu but it also makes wonderfully tasty pizza crust.

Traditional recipes say polenta needs to be stirred and stirred and stirred as it cooks but I find the cover-and-forget-it approach much easier to handle on a weeknight. This is a method made famous by Marcella Hazan, and it's become my favorite polenta making method too.

The idea is to get the polenta going by whisking coarse-ground polenta or yellow cornmeal into boiling water and stirring until it gets thick. You then cover the pot and just let the polenta cook while you make the rest of dinner. Every 10 minutes or so, uncover the pot and give it a good stir to make sure it's cooking evenly and the sides aren't drying out. Thirty to forty minutes later, your polenta is cooked and ready to eat!

After it has cooked for about 15minutes, the polenta can look done and if at this point if you taste it and like it, by all means serve it! But if you can be just a little more patient and let it cook for a little longer, you'll find that the polenta tastes sweeter and more deeply corn-like, and that any last grittiness from the ground corn has mellowed out and you have polenta with a wonderfully silken texture. I love it at 30 minutes, but you can also cook it a little longer if you have time or want a thicker polenta.

If you're really craving creamy polenta again, you can warm the leftovers with some water or milk, and stir until it becomes soft again. Or, since you now know how easy it is, you can just make another batch.

Creamy Stovetop Polenta

Ingredients

4 cups water or stock

1 teaspoon kosher salt

1 cup polenta or yellow cornmeal

1 cup Parmigiano-Reggiano, Parmesan or Romano cheese (optional)

1-3 Tablespoons butter or extra virgin olive oil (optional

Directions:

I n a 2-3 quart saucepan, bring water or stock to a brisk boil. Add salt.

Gradually add the polenta to the water by allowing it to fall in a steady stream between your fingers into the pot like sand through your fingers, while whisking gently. Adding the polenta or cornmeal to the pot in this way will prevent lumping.

Using a whisk, continue stirring until polenta has thickened. Reduce the heat to low and continue stirring until the polenta has thickened enough so the unincorporated polenta grains don't settle back onto the bottom of the pan when you stop stirring.

At this point, the cornmeal and liquid should be thoroughly combined.

Cover the polenta and continue cooking. Remove cover and stir vigorously every 10 minutes or so, making sure to scrape the sides, and bottom, of the pan. Replace cover. Cook 30 minutes for softer polenta with the consistency of mashed potatoes or 40 minutes for thicker polenta.

Stir in cheese and butter, if using. Serve immediately, or cover the pan, turn off the burner and let the polenta sit up to 15 minutes before serving.

Notes:

You can add 1/2 of a small, finely diced onion to the water or stock as it's coming to a boil.

To reheat polenta, warm it with a little broth, milk, or water, and stir vigorously. It won't be quite as creamy as it was originally, but it should still be pourable.

Alternatively, pour the polenta into a flat baking dish where it will cool and become firm.

After is has cooled and become firm, it can be cut in triangles and grilled, pan fried in olive oil or butter or oven baked for 20 minutes.

If you bake polenta in a sheet pan, it makes a delicious pizza crust. Just bake it, add your toppings and bake it again for 20 minutes or so.

Polenta can grilled and sliced and topped with sautéed mushrooms, eggplant slices, goats cheese, etc.

Stir all the time, and if you have used too much of the flour and the mixture is too thick, add a little water.

When the polenta is smooth and does not taste of raw maize, it is ready.

Another trick to telling when polenta is done is when it comes away cleanly from the sides of the pot. That may make it a little easier to tell when it's done.

For me, grilled polenta is good with baked or fried fish nuggets and lumps of Parmesan cheese.

After you have poured the polenta into a pan or container, some will remain stuck to the sides of the pot. Let it dry, even as long as a day, and peel these skins off. They are delicious with parmesan cheese.

I hope this information helps you make perfect polenta with ease! It's at least as comforting as mashed potatoes and easier!

Nutritional Facts:

Serving Size: 1 (226 g)

Servings Per Recipe: 8

Amount Per Serving:

Calories: 165.6	Sodium: 23.1 mg
Calories from Fat: 14	Total Carbs: 35.1 g
Total Fat: 1.6 g	Fiber: 3.3 g
Sat. Fat: 0.2 g	Sugars: 0.2 g
Cholesterol: 0.0 mg	Protein: 3.7 g

Citrus Salmon

Total Time: 1 hour, 30 minutes

Prep Time: 5 minutes

Cook Time: 1 hour, 30 minutes

Servings: 6

Ingredients:

1 1/2 pounds salmon fillets

Kosher salt

Freshly ground white pepper to taste

1/4 cup freshly squeezed lemon juice

1 teaspoon toasted sesame oil

2 teaspoons tamari

A few drops of hot sauce

1 clove garlic, minced

1/2 cup scallions, sliced

5 Tablespoons fresh parsley, chopped

1 Tablespoon extra virgin olive oil

2 teaspoons lemon zest

2 teaspoons orange zest

Orange and lemon slices, for garnish

Parsley, chopped, for garnish

Directions:

Butter slow cooker; and add lemon juice, sesame oil, tamari, hot sauce and garlic to slow cooker.

Sprinkle salmon fillets with salt and pepper. Place fish in slow cooker.

Drizzle olive oil over salmon, top with scallions, parsley, orange and lemon zest.

Cover and cook on Low for 3 1/2 hours.

Transfer salmon to serving platter and remove skin.

Serve garnished with orange and lemon slices and sprigs of fresh parsley.

This is excellent served with rice pilaf or egg noodles.

Nutrition Facts:

Serving Size 143 g

Amount Per Serving

Calories:270	Sodium: 213mg
Calories from Fat: 155	Total Carbs:1.6g
Total Fat: 17.2g	Fiber:0.5g
Sat. Fat:3.4g	Sugars:0.5g
Cholesterol: 71mg	Protein: 25.6g

Salmon with Mango Avocado Salsa

Total Time: 3 1/2 hrs. 25 mins.

Prep Time: 25 mins.

Cook Time: 3 1/2 hrs.

Servings: 6

Ingredients:

1 1/2 lbs. salmon fillets

1/4 cup cilantro stems removed, chopped

2 cloves garlic, minced

2-3 Tablespoons freshly squeezed lime juice

2 Tablespoons extra virgin olive oil

1/4 teaspoon kosher salt

Freshly ground white pepper

Mango Avocado Salsa, recipe follows

Directions:

Coat slow cooker with olive oil.

Place fillets, skin side down, in slow cooker.

Top with cilantro.

In a small bowl combine, garlic, lime juice, olive oil, salt and white pepper.

Pour mixture over salmon.

Cook on Low 3 1/2 hours.

Transfer salmon to serving platter and remove skin.

Pour juices over the top and serve with Mango Avocado Salsa.

Nutrition Facts:

Serving Size 120 g

Amount Per Serving

Calories:275	Cholesterol: 71mg
Calories from Fat:168	Sodium:167mg
Total Fat:18.7g	Total Carbs:0.4g
Sat. Fat:3.5g	Protein:25.1g

Mango Avocado Salsa

Total Time: 15 min

Prep time: 15 min

Serves: 4 to 6

Ingredients

1 mango, peeled and diced

1 avocado, peeled and diced

1/2 cup cucumber, peeled, diced

1 Tablespoon jalapeno, finely chopped

1/3 cup red onion, diced

1/4 cup red bell pepper, diced

1 Tablespoon freshly squeezed lime juice

1/3 cup cilantro leaves, roughly chopped

Kosher salt and pepper

Directions

Combine the mango, avocado, cucumber, jalapeno, red onion, red bell pepper, lime juice and cilantro leaves and stir to combine.

Season with salt and pepper.

Nutrition Facts:

Serving Size 96 g

Amount Per Serving

Calories: 104	Sodium: 4mg
Calories from Fat: 68	Carbs: 7.8g
Total Fat:7.6g	Fiber: 3.6g
Sat. Fat: 0.8g	Sugars: 6.4g
Cholesterol: 0mg	Protein: 1.1g

Salmon with Asparagus

Total Time: 3 hrs. 45 mins.

Prep Time: 15 mins.

Cook Time: 3hrs.30 mins.

Servings:6

Ingredients:

1/2 cup water

1/2 cup chicken broth

1 cup dry white wine

1/2 small onion, thinly sliced

3 sprigs tarragon, plus 1 teaspoon minced tarragon leaves

1/2 teaspoon kosher salt

Freshly ground white pepper

1 1/2 lbs. salmon fillets

11/2 lbs. fresh asparagus spears, trimmed

1 Tablespoon butter

1 Tablespoon olive oil

1 large shallot, minced

2 teaspoons white wine vinegar

Directions:

Combine the water, broth, wine, onion, tarragon sprigs salt and white pepper in the slow cooker. Stir, cover and cook on Low for 30 minutes.

Add the salmon fillets. Cover and cook on Low for 3 hours or until salmon is opaque and tender.

Transfer the salmon to a serving platter, and remove the skin. Cover loosely to keep warm.

Discard the braising liquid and tarragon sprigs.

During the last 30 minutes of salmon cooking time, over high heat, bring a large pot of lightly salted water to a boil.

Add asparagus spears and cook for about 4 minutes, or until crisp-tender. Immediately pour into a colander in the sink and rinse well under cold running water. Spread on a clean dish towel or paper towels to dry.

Just before serving, heat butter and oil in a large skillet over medium heat until hot but not smoking. Add the shallot and cook for 2 or 3 minutes, or until slightly softened but not browned.

Add asparagus spears and stir to coat and warm through, then add the vinegar and minced tarragon, tossing to incorporate.

Arrange asparagus spears around salmon fillets.

Serve warm or at room temperature.

Serve with parslied new red potatoes.

Nutrition Facts:

Serving Size 601 g

Amount Per Serving

Calories: 392	Sodium: 351mg
Calories from Fat: 170	Total Carbs: 17.8g
Total Fat: 18.9g	Fiber:8.9g
Sat. Fat; 4.6g	Sugars: 8.4g
Cholesterol: 77mg	Protein:34.7g

Shrimp Marinara

Total Time: 7-8 hours 20 mins.

Prep Time: 5 mins.

Cook Time: 7-8 hours

Servings: 6-8

This is an easy marinara sauce for the slow cooker, great over hot cooked pasta.

Ingredients:

1 (28 oz.) can ground, peeled tomatoes

1 (12 oz.) can tomato paste

1/2 cup dry red wine

1/4 cup fresh parsley, minced

4 cloves garlic, minced

1 1/2 tsp. dried basil

2 teaspoon dried oregano

1 teaspoon kosher salt

1/4 teaspoon freshly ground black pepper

1/2 teaspoon seasoned salt

2 lb. medium shrimp, shelled, cooked and thawed if frozen

Grated Parmesan cheese, for garnish

Directions:

Combine tomatoes, tomato paste, red wine, parsley, garlic, basil, , oregano, salt, pepper and seasoned salt in slow cooker.

Cover and cook on Low for 7-8 hours.

Raise temperature to High, stir in cooked shrimp, cover and cook on high for about 15 minutes, or until just heated through.

Serve over pasta, spaghetti squash, or polenta with a big green salad..

Pass Parmesan cheese at the table.

Nutrition Facts:

Serving Size 367 g

Amount Per Serving

Calories: 243	Carbs:18.4g
Calories from Fat:19	Fiber: 4.6g
Total Fat:2.1g	Sugars: 9.1g
Cholesterol:297mg	Protein:35.1g
Sodium:1294mg	

Foil Wrapped Lemon Pepper Sole with Asparagus

Total Time: 4 hrs. 15 mins.

Prep Time: 15 mins.

Cook Time: 4 hrs.

Servings 4

You can substitute just about any fish filet for the sole. Fresh broccoli or fresh green beans are excellent substitutes for the asparagus.

Ingredients:

1 bunch asparagus, trimmed

1 1/2 lbs. sole filets, thawed if frozen

1/2 cup freshly squeezed lemon juice

Lemon Pepper Seasoning

1/2 Tablespoon extra virgin olive oil for each packet

Directions:

You will need a piece of foil for each serving large enough to completely wrap contents.

Portion sole into 4 even portions and place each portion in the center of sheet of foil and season with lemon pepper seasoning using approximately 1/4 teaspoon per packet. Add 2 Tablespoons lemon juice and 1/2 Tablespoon of olive oil.

Divide asparagus into 4 equal portions. Top sole with asparagus.

Fold the sides of the foil over the sole and fold to close and fold the ends of the foil up to form a packet. This should form a tightly wrapped packet.

Repeat this process with the remaining 3 portions

Place packets in the slow cooker, stacking if necessary.

Cover and cook on High for 4 hours.

Nutrition Facts:

Serving Size 217 g

Amount Per Serving:

Calories:213	Sodium:125mg
Calories from Fat;81	Carbs:3.4g
Total Fat:9.0g	Fiber:1.7g
Sat. Fat:1.6g	Sugars:1.8g
Cholesterol:77mg	Protein:29.2g

Slow Cooker Chicken and Shrimp

Total Time: 6-8 hrs, 40 mins.

Prep Time: 20 mins

Cook Time: 6-8 hrs. 20 mins.

Serves: 4

Ingredients:

1 lb. boneless, skinless chicken thighs

1/2 teaspoon kosher salt

1/8 teaspoon freshly ground black pepper

1/2 teaspoon crushed red pepper flakes

2 onions, chopped

6 cloves garlic, minced

1 (14 oz.) can seasoned diced tomatoes, undrained

1 (8oz.) can tomato sauce

3 Tablespoons tomato paste

1 cup chicken broth

1 teaspoon dried thyme leaves

1/2 teaspoon dried basil leaves

3 Tablespoons lemon juice

1 (8 oz.) package frozen cooked shrimp, thawed

1 (12 oz.) can quartered artichoke hearts, drained

1 Tablespoon cornstarch

2/3 cup crumbled feta cheese

Directions:

Cut chicken into large chunks and season with salt and pepper to taste.

 Place onion and garlic in bottom slow cooker and top with chicken.

In a medium bowl, combine diced tomatoes, tomato sauce, tomato paste, chicken broth, thyme, basil, and lemon juice and mix well. Pour over chicken.

Cover slow cooker and cook on low for 6-8 hours until chicken is tender with the juices running clear or 165°F.on a thermometer.

Stir in thawed and drained shrimp and artichoke hearts

Place cornstarch in a small bowl and add 2 Tablespoons water. Stir well to blend. Pour into slow cooker.

Cover and cook for 15-20 minutes or until heated through and slightly thickened.

Serve over hot cooked pasta or couscous and sprinkle with feta cheese.

Nutrition Facts:

Serving Size 766 g

Amount Per Serving:

Calories:369	Sodium:701mg
Calories from Fat:100	Total Carbs:29.8g
Total Fat:11.1g	Fiber:7.8g
Sat. Fat:4.4g	Sugars:17.4g
Cholesterol:162mg	Protein:39.5g

Poached Swordfish with Lemon-Parsley Sauce

Total Time: 1 hrs. 30 mins.

Prep Time: 15 mins.

Cook Time: 1 hr.15 mins.

Servings: 4

Swordfish steaks are usually cut thicker than most fish fillets, and they're a firmer fish so it takes longer to poach them. You can speed up the poaching process a little if you remove the steaks from the refrigerator and let them sit at room-temperature for 30 minutes before adding to slow cooker.

Ingredients:

1 Tablespoon butter

4 thin slices sweet onion

2 cups water

4 (6-ounce) swordfish steaks

Kosher salt, to taste

1 lemon, thinly sliced, seeds removed

6 Tablespoons extra-virgin olive oil

3 Tablespoons fresh lemon juice

3/4 teaspoon Dijon mustard

Freshly ground white pepper, to taste

3 Tablespoons fresh flat leaf parsley, minced

8 cups baby salad greens or mesclun mix

Directions:

Butter the bottom and halfway up the side of the slow cooker.

Arrange onion slices over the bottom of the slow cooker, pressing them into the butter so that they stay in place. Pour in the water. Cover and cook on high for 30 minutes.

Salt and white pepper swordfish steaks, to taste and place on onion slices. Top with lemon slices.

Cover and cook on high for 45 minutes or until the fish is opaque. Remove from slow cooker and either wrap to keep warm or chill in fridge.

In a bowl, combine oil, lemon juice, mustard, and white pepper, whisk to combine and fold in the parsley. Evenly divide the sauce between the swordfish steaks.

Toss 8 cups of salad greens with 2/3 of dressing. Arrange 2 cups of greens on each of 4 individual plates.

Place a hot or chilled swordfish steak on top of each plate of dressed greens.

Spoon the remaining sauce over the fish.

Nutrition Facts:

Serving Size 299 g

Amount Per Serving:

Calories:330	Sodium:189mg
Calories from Fat:199	Total Carbs:3.2g
Total Fat:22.1g	Fiber:1.8g
Sat. Fat:4.9g	Sugars;1.3g
Cholesterol:62mg	Protein:29.9g

Easy Cheesy Salmon Loaf

Total Time: 3-5 hrs. 35 mins.

Prep Time: 15 mins

Cook Time: 3 hrs. 20 mins.

Serves: 4

You can cook this recipe in the crock pot as directed or bake in conventional oven at 350°F. for 25 minutes.

Salmon bones may be left in, if desired, for additional calcium if the salmon is mashed with the back of a spoon.

Ingredients:

1 Tablespoon extra virgin olive oil

1 (8 oz.) package sliced mushrooms

1 small onion, minced

1 (16 oz.) can salmon, drained

1 1/2 cups fresh breadcrumbs

2 eggs, beaten

1 cup grated cheddar cheese

1 Tablespoon lemon juice

1/4 teaspoon dry mustard

1 teaspoon Worcestershire sauce

1/2 teaspoon kosher salt

1 (10 oz.) package frozen peas, thawed, optional

Directions:

Cut three 24-in. x 3-in. strips of heavy duty foil; crisscross so they resemble spokes of a wheel. Place strips on the bottom and up the sides of a slow cooker coated with cooking spray.

In a medium sauté pan, heat olive oil, add mushrooms and onion and sauté until vegetables are soft and liquid has evaporated.

Flake fish in bowl, removing all bones.

Add all remaining ingredients, including sautéed vegetables, excepting peas, and mix thoroughly.

Pour into lightly greased crock pot or casserole dish and shape into rounded loaf, pulling the foil strips up the side of the slow cooker so they can act as handles for removing salmon loaf.

Cover and cook on High 1 hour then reduce to Low and cook for an additional 3 to 5 hours.

If desired, top salmon loaf with optional peas during the last hour of cooking.

Nutrition Facts:

Serving Size 192 g

Amount Per Serving:

Calories:394	Sodium:393mg
Calories from Fat:189	Carbs:22.3g
Total Fat:21.0g	Fiber:1.9g
Sat. Fat:7.0g	Sugars:3.2g
Cholesterol:122mg	Protein: 28.2g

Slow-Cooker Halibut Stew

Total Time: 8-9 hrs. 20 mins.

Prep Time: 20 mins.

Cook Time: 8-9 hrs.

Servings: 6

Ingredients:

1 red bell pepper, cut into 3/4" pieces

1 small yellow onion, roughly chopped

2 carrots, thinly sliced

1 stalk celery, thinly sliced

1 large potato, peeled, cut into 1" pieces

1 1/2 cups clam broth or chicken stock

2 Tablespoons freshly squeezed lime juice

3 cloves garlic, minced

1/2 teaspoon freshly ground black pepper

Kosher salt to taste

1 teaspoon chili powder

1/4 cup cilantro, chopped

1/2 teaspoon cumin

1/2 teaspoon red pepper flakes

1 pound halibut fillets, thawed if frozen, rinsed and cut into bite size pieces

Cilantro, for garnish

Lime wedges, for garnish

Directions:

Combine all the above ingredients in slow-cooker, except halibut and garnishes.

Cover and cook on Low 8-9 hours.

During the last 30 minutes of cooking time add halibut pieces, cover and cook until halibut is opaque. .

Garnish with additional cilantro if desired.

Nutrition Facts:

Serving Size 226 g

Amount Per Serving:

Calories: 148	Sodium: 296 mg
Total Fat: 2 g	Carbs: 12 g
Sat. Fats: 1 g	Fiber: 2 g
Trans Fats: 0 g	Sugars: 4 g
Cholesterol: 26 mg	Protein: 18 g

Salmon and Green Beans

Total Time: 3-4 hrs.1 5 mins.

Prep Time: 15 mins.

Cook Time: 3-4 hrs.

Servings: 4

Ingredients:

1 1/4 lbs. salmon, thawed if frozen

1 lb. fresh green beans, washed and tips removed

1/4 cup tamari

1/4 cup honey

1 clove garlic, finely minced

Freshly ground white pepper, to taste

1 Tablespoon fresh ginger, finely minced

1/4 cup freshly squeezed lemon juice

1/4 cup freshly squeezed blood orange juice or substitute freshly squeezed orange juice

Directions:

In a small bowl, combine tamari, honey, garlic, ginger, citrus juices and white pepper.

Wash and trim green beans, place in slow cooker

Place fish on top of green beans.

Pour liquid mixture over the top.

Cover and cook on Low for 3-4 hours

Transfer salmon and green beans to a serving platter. Remove skin from salmon and drizzle juices over the top,

Serve with quinoa or brown rice.

Nutrition Facts:

Serving Size 218 g

Amount Per Serving:

Calories:279	Sodium:736mg
Calories from Fat:107	Carbs:19.8g
Total Fat:11.9g	Fiber:2.9g
Sat. Fat:2.5g	Sugars:14.0g
Cholesterol: 60mg	Protein:23.8g

Slow Cooker Poached Salmon

Total Time: 55 mins.

Prep Time: 10 mins.

Cook Time: 45mins

Servings: 4

Ingredients:

2 cups water

1 cup dry white wine

1 onion, sliced

1 lemon, sliced

1 sprig fresh dill

1 teaspoon kosher salt

1 1/2 lbs. salmon fillets

Horseradish Sauce (recipe follows)

Directions:

In the slow cooker, combine water and wine and heat on High for 30 minutes.

Add the onion slices, lemon slices, dill, salt, and salmon.

Cover and cook on High for about 40 minutes or until the salmon is opaque and cooked through.

Serve hot or cold with horseradish sauce.

If serving hot, serve with mashed potatoes and steamed broccoli.

If serving cold, make a tossed salad and add fresh dill and baby red potatoes to the salad. Top the salad with the halibut and use the Horseradish sauce as dressing.

Nutrition Facts:

Serving Size 258 g

Amount Per Serving:

Calories:410	Sodium:688mg
Calories from Fat:189	Carbs:4.1g
Total Fat:21.0g	Fiber:0.6g
Sat. Fat:4.3g	Sugars:1.6g
Cholesterol:107mg	Protein:37.9g

Horseradish Sauce
Makes about 2 cups

Ingredients

1 1/2 cups low fat sour cream or yogurt

1/2 cup prepared horseradish

6 Tablespoons chopped fresh chives

4 teaspoons fresh lemon juice

Directions:

In small bowl, whisk all ingredients to combine.

Season with kosher salt and freshly ground white pepper.

Can be prepared 2 days in advance. Cover and chill.

Nutrition Facts:

Serving Size 65 g

Amount Per Serving:

Calories:70	Sodium:66mg
Calories from Fat:50	Total Carbs:3.8g
Total Fat:5.6g	Fiber:0.6g
Sat. Fat:3.4g	Sugars:1.4g
Cholesterol:18mg	Protein:1.6g

Vegetable Ragout with Cornmeal Crusted Halibut Nuggets

Total Time: 4-10 hrs. 25 mins.

Prep Time: 25 mins.

Cook Time: 4-10 hrs.

Servings: 4-6

This delicious stew is a meal in itself. All it needs is crusty bread to mop up the sauce.

This dish can also be made on top of the stove, reducing cooking times and using low heat to gently simmer the dish.

Ingredients:

1 Tablespoon extra virgin olive oil

2 onions, finely chopped

2 carrots, peeled and finely chopped

1 teaspoon, dried oregano

1 teaspoon kosher salt

1/2 teaspoon freshly ground black pepper

2 cups, bottled clam juice or chicken stock

2 cups dry vermouth or dry white wine

2 cups, water

1 Tablespoon freshly squeezed lime juice

2 potatoes cut into 1/2 inch dice

1 sweet potato, cut in 1" dice

1 red bell pepper, coarsely chopped

1/2 cup yellow cornmeal

1 teaspoon chili powder

1/4 teaspoon cayenne pepper

Kosher salt and freshly ground black pepper, to taste

1 1/2 pounds, halibut, cut into 1/2-inch pieces

2 Tablespoons extra virgin olive oil, for frying halibut

Sour cream, garnish

Lime wedges, garnish

Directions:

In a large sauté pan, heat the 1 Tablespoon of oil over medium heat until hot but not smoking.

Add chopped onions carrots and celery. Cook, stirring, until the carrots are softened, about 7 minutes.

Add oregano, salt and pepper and cook, stirring, for 1 minute.

Transfer to slow cooker. Add clam juice or broth, vermouth, water and lime juice.

Add the potatoes and sweet potatoes and stir to combine.

Cover and cook on Low for 8-10 hours or on High for 4-5 hours, or until vegetables are tender.

Stir in the bell pepper. Cover the pot once again and cook on High for 20 minutes or until the bell pepper is soft.

In a zip top plastic bag, combine cornmeal and chili powder. Add the halibut pieces and toss gently until the pieces are evenly coated.

In a medium sauté pan, heat the remaining 2 tablespoons olive oil over medium-high heat until hot but not smoking. Add halibut pieces, in batches if necessary, and sauté, turning once, until the fish pieces are nicely browned.

Discard any excess cornmeal mixture.

Ladle the stew into individual serving bowls and top with browned halibut nuggets'

Top with a dollop of sour cream, add a lime wedge and serve.

Nutrition Facts:

Serving Size 425 g

Amount Per Serving:

Calories:430	Sodium: 506mg
Calories from Fat:100	Total Carbs:33.9g
Total Fat:11.1g	Fiber:5.5g
Sat. Fat:1.6g	Sugars:7.3g
Cholesterol:46mg	Protein:35.0g

Salmon with Lemon and Green Olive Sauce

Total Time: 6 hrs. 5 mins.

Prep Time: 5 mins.

Cook Time: 6 hrs.

Servings: 6

Ingredients:

Extra virgin olive oil for coating slow cooker

1 large lemon, thinly sliced and seeds removed

2 medium shallots, thinly sliced

1/2 cup water

1 1/2 pounds thick salmon fillet, cut in 6 pieces

2 Tablespoons extra virgin olive oil

Kosher salt and freshly ground black pepper

Sauce:

2 Tablespoons extra virgin olive oil

1 Tablespoon freshly squeezed lemon juice

1/2 teaspoon lemon zest

1/2 teaspoon dried oregano

Kosher salt and freshly ground black pepper

1/2 cup pitted green olives, chopped

1 Tablespoon fresh flat leaf parsley, chopped

1 Tablespoon capers, rinsed

Directions:

Coat bottom and sides of slow cooker with extra virgin olive oil.

Drop half of the shallots into the bottom of slow cooker. Add half the lemon slices and water.

Rub the salmon with olive oil and sprinkle with salt and pepper, to taste.

Place salmon skin side down in the slow cooker. Top with remaining lemon slices and shallot.

Cover and cook on Low for 60-75 minutes, or until the salmon is opaque and cooked through.

While salmon is cooking, make the sauce:

In a small bowl, whisk together, olive oil, lemon juice, zest, oregano, salt and pepper to taste. Stir in olives, parsley and capers.

Transfer salmon to individual plates, remove skin and drizzle with sauce.

This is scrumptious served hot with couscous or polenta and a big green salad.

It's also wonderful served at room temperature on a bed of baby greens accompanied by a loaf of crusty bread.

Nutrition Facts:

Serving Size 152 g

Amount Per Serving:

Calories:318	Cholesterol:71mg
Calories from Fat:210	Sodium:113mg
Total Fat:23.4g	Carbs:0.8g
Sat Fat:4.2g	Protein:25.2g

Salmon with Dill and Shallots

Total Time: 6 hrs. 5 mins.

Prep Time: 5 mins.

Cook Time: 6 hrs.

Servings: 6

Ingredients:

4 large shallots, thinly sliced

1/4 cup dry white wine

1 cup water

1 1/2 lbs. boneless salmon fillet

1 Tablespoon extra virgin olive oil

Kosher salt and freshly ground black pepper, to taste

2 Tablespoons freshly squeezed lemon juice

3 or 4 sprigs fresh dill, chopped or 1/2 tsp. dried dill weed

1 lemon, sliced and seeds removed

Directions:

Rinse salmon on both sides and pat dry with paper towel. With skin side down, cut into 6 even portions.

Sprinkle shallots in bottom of slow cooker. Pour wine and water over.

Mix oil and dill together and spoon over the top of salmon. Rub oil in to make sure salmon is evenly coated with oil.

Place salmon pieces in slow cooker, skin side down. Add lemon juice and season with salt and pepper.

Top with lemon slices and cover and cook on Low for 90 minutes.

Gently remove salmon from slow cooker with slotted spatula. Remove skin.

Serve warm with thyme roasted sweet potatoes and a green salad.

Nutrition Facts:

Serving Size 208 g

Amount Per Serving:

Calories:341	Cholesterol:95mg
Calories from Fat:189	Sodium:95mg
Total Fat:21.0g	Total Carbs:0.4g
Sat Fat:4.2g	Protein:33.5g

Thyme-Roasted Sweet Potatoes

Total Time: 50 mins.

Prep Time: 10 mins.

Cook Time: 40 mins.

Servings: 6

Ingredients:

4 medium sweet potatoes, peeled and cut into thick chunks

3 Tablespoons extra virgin olive oil

2 Tablespoons Balsamic vinegar

4 large cloves garlic, minced

1/3 cup fresh thyme leaves or 1 teaspoon of dried thyme leaves

1/2 teaspoon kosher salt

1/2 teaspoon crushed red pepper flakes

6 thyme sprigs for garnish

Directions:

Preheat oven to 425°F.

In large mixing bowl, combine all ingredients and toss.

Arrange potatoes in single layer on heavyweight rimmed baking sheet or in 13x9-inch baking dish.

Place on top rack of oven and roast until tender and slightly browned, about 40 minutes. Serve warm or at room temperature, garnished with thyme sprigs.

Variation: Instead of 4 medium sweet potatoes, use 2 large sweet potatoes, 2 large sweet white onions, and 2 large red bell peppers.

Increase crushed red pepper flakes to 3/4 teaspoons, and bake for 1 hour, instead of 40 minutes.

This is a delicious vegetable side dish or served over polenta, it can also be a vegetarian entrée!

Nutrition Facts:

Serving Size 116 g

Amount Per Serving:

Calories:187	Sodium:205mg
Calories from Fat:67	Total Carbs:29.7g
Total Fat:7.4g	Fiber:5.1g
Sat Fat:1.1g	Sugars:0.6g
Cholesterol:0mg	Protein:1.8g

Vegetarian:

Vegetarian Stuffed Peppers

Total Time: 6 hrs. 20 mins.

Prep Time: 20 mins.

Cook Time: 6 hrs.

Yield: 5 peppers

Serves: 5

These are super easy to make. Plan ahead. Cook rice for a meal a few days in advance and cook enough for this recipe at the same time. You can substitute just about any cooked grain for the rice. Try using quinoa, barley or even whole oats (not oatmeal). This is also a great recipe for using up odds and ends of leftover vegetables. Just toss them into the filling!

As a variation of this recipe, substitute Feta cheese for Parmesan cheese and add a 10oz. package of thawed, chopped spinach which has been well drained.

Ingredients:

5 red or green bell peppers or a combination of the two colors

2 cups brown rice, cooked

2 Tablespoons extra virgin olive oil

3 portabella mushroom caps, diced fine

1 medium onion, diced

2 garlic cloves, minced

1 teaspoon dried oregano

2 Tablespoons dry red or white wine

1 Tablespoon tamari

1/4 cup parmesan cheese

1/2 teaspoon kosher salt

1/2 teaspoon freshly ground black pepper

1 (32 ounce) jar marinara sauce

Directions:

Cut tops off bell peppers. Remove seeds and inner membrane.

In a large sauté pan, heat the olive oil until hot but not smoking. Add the onions and sauté until translucent.

Add the mushrooms and sauté until most of the moisture has evaporated.

Add garlic and oregano and sauté for 30 seconds or so.

Push everything in the pan to the side to make a well in the center. Add the wine and cook for 2 minutes to reduce slightly. Stir contents of the pan together, remove from heat and set aside.

In a medium bowl, stir together rice, mushroom mixture, cheese, tamari, salt and pepper.

Stuff peppers.

Pour half of the marinara into the slow cooker, carefully lay peppers on top, then carefully pour remaining sauce over the top..

Cover and cook on low for 6 hours.

Nutritional Facts:

Serving Size: 1 (488 g)

Servings Per Recipe: 5

Amount Per Serving:

Calories: 352.1	Sodium: 1163.5 mg
Calories from Fat: 73	Carbs: 58.8 g
Total Fat: 8.1 g	Fiber: 10.4 g
Sat. Fat: 2.5 g	Sugars: 25.4 g
Cholesterol: 8.5 mg	Protein: 10.0 g

Tex-Mex Lentils

Total Time: 8 hrs. 10 mins.

Prep Time: 10 mins.

Cook Time: 8 hrs.

Servings: 12

Here's another ridiculously simple little recipe that came to mind as I was writing the stuffed pepper recipe. This is a versatile base recipe that has many uses. A good example is to cut the rice in the stuffed pepper recipe in half and add 1 cup of this mixture in place of 1 cup of rice.

This is a great vegetarian filling for tacos, topping for taco salads or combined with some avocado slices and vegetables makes a delicious burrito!

You can combine this with some bow tie pasta, extra virgin olive oil, the juice of 1 lemon, lemon zest, and some fresh vegetables such as tomatoes and scallions and have a healthy pasta salad.

Ingredients:

1 cup onion, chopped

2 cloves garlic, minced

1 teaspoon extra virgin olive oil

1 cup dry lentils, picked over, debris removed and washed well under cold water

1 Tablespoon chili powder

2 teaspoons ground cumin

1 teaspoon oregano

14 oz. vegetable stock

1 teaspoon tamari

1 cup salsa

Directions:

Put everything in the slow cooker and cook on high for 8-12 hours, stirring occasionally, adding more stock or water as needed.

Nutritional Facts:

Serving Size: 1 (85 g)

Servings Per Recipe: 12

Amount Per Serving:

Calories: 74.5	Sodium: 143.5 mg
Calories from Fat: 6	Total Carbs: 12.8 g
Total Fat: 0.7 g	Fiber: 5.7 g
Sat. Fat: 0.0 g	Sugars: 1.6 g
Cholesterol: 0.0 mg	Protein: 4.7 g

North African Squash-Eggplant Casserole

Total Time: 9 hrs. 30 mins.

Prep Time: 30 mins.

Cook Time: 9 hrs.

Servings: 10

Butternut squash can be very difficult to peel. I find it's easier to peel if you cut it into 1" or so thick slices before attempting to peel. It's also available in the market already peeled as a seasonal item available in the fall and winter. Almost any variety of winter squash will work in this recipe with the exception of Blue Hubbard which will disintegrate with the long cook time.

Ingredients:

1 butternut squash, peeled, seeded, cubed

2 cups Japanese eggplant, cubed (the long, thin, striated purple & white ones)

2 cups zucchini, cubed

10 oz. frozen okra, thawed

1 onion, chopped

1 carrot, sliced

1 (8 oz.) can tomato sauce

1/2 cup vegetable stock

1/3 cup raisins

1 clove garlic, minced

1/2 teaspoon cumin

1/2 teaspoon turmeric

1/4 teaspoon crushed red pepper flakes

1/4 teaspoon cinnamon

1/4 teaspoon paprika

Directions:

Layer the squash, eggplant, zucchini, okra, onion and carrot in the slow cooker in the order listed.

Mix together the remaining ingredients and pour into slow cooker.

Cover and cook on low for 7-9 hours or until vegetables are tender..

Nutritional Facts:

Serving Size: 1 (228 g)

Servings Per Recipe: 10

Amount Per Serving:

Calories: 97.9	Sodium: 133.3 mg
Calories from Fat: 3	Carbs: 24.4 g
Total Fat: 0.4 g	Fiber: 4.6 g
Sat. Fat: 0.0 g	Sugars 8.7 g
Cholesterol: 0.0 mg	Protein 2.7 g

Easy Ratatouille

Total Time: 9 hrs. 30 mins.

Prep Time: 30 mins.

Cook Time: 9 hrs.

Serves: 8

Ratatouille is a colorful French dish which combines many sweet vegetables such as peppers, tomatoes, onions and zucchini. The vegetables are stewed together in a gravy of olive oil, garlic and herbs. As usual, the slow cooker is a big time saver, reducing the normal hour of prep time to about 30 minutes.

Most often Ratatouille is eaten as a vegetarian entree, or in omelette, with bread, polenta, pasta or rice. I like it as a pizza topping for a pizza with a polenta crust. It can also be served as a side dish with meat for non-vegetarians.

Ingredients:

8 Tablespoons extra virgin olive oil, divided

4 cloves garlic, minced

2 large onions, chopped

5 small Japanese eggplants, unpeeled, cut into 3/4" dice (the long, thin, striated purple & white ones)

2 yellow bell peppers, chopped

1 orange bell pepper, chopped

1 red bell pepper, chopped

3 zucchini squash, diced

4 oz. Kalamata olives, pitted

1 (28oz.) can San Marzano tomatoes, undrained

1 Tablespoon fresh tarragon

Kosher salt, to taste

Freshly ground black pepper

Directions:

In a large sauté pan heat 2 Tbsp. olive oil over medium high heat until hot but not smoking. (of the 1/4 cup. Add more as needed.) Add the onions and sauté for about 5 minutes. Add the garlic, cook for 30 seconds, add eggplant, stir to coat with oil, cover, reduce heat, and cook for about 10 minutes or until the eggplant is tender

Transfer the contents of the sauté pan to the slow cooker.

"Smoosh" the tomatoes up with your fingers, reserving juice and add the tomatoes and juice to the slow cooker along with bell peppers, zucchini, olives, spices and 4 tablespoons of olive oil. Stir well, cover and cook on High for about 6 hours.

Serve with Parmesan cheese passed at the table.

Nutrition Facts:

Serving Size 651 g

Amount Per Serving:

Calories: 412	Sodium: 322mg
Calories from Fat: 262	Carbs: 38.1g
Total Fat: 29.1g	Fiber: 18.0g
Sat. Fat: 4.0g	Sugars: 18.5g
Cholesterol: 0mg	Protein: 7.7g

Mediterranean Eggplant

Total Time: 4 hrs. 10 mins.

Prep Time: 10 mins.

Cook Time: 4 hrs.

Serves: 4-6

Ingredients:

1 1/2 lbs. Japanese eggplant, cubed, skin on (the long, thin, striated purple & white ones)

2 medium onions, cut in half and sliced thin

3 celery ribs, rough diced

2 yellow summer squash, cut in 3/4" dice

2 zucchini squash, cut in 3/4" dice

3 Tablespoons extra virgin olive oil

2 cups diced Italian tomatoes, with juice

1/4 cup tomato sauce

1/2 cup Kalamata olives, pitted

2 Tablespoons balsamic vinegar

1/4 cup vegetable stock

1 Tablespoon sugar

1 -2 Tablespoons capers

1 teaspoon dried oregano

2 Tablespoons fresh basil, minced

Kosher salt, to taste

Freshly ground black pepper, to taste

Feta cheese, optional garnish

Extra virgin olive oil for drizzling at the table.

Directions:

In slow cooker layer eggplant, onion, celery, olive oil, tomatoes, tomato sauce, stock, oregano, salt and pepper and mix well. Top with the olives and squash but don't stir. Cover and cook on Low for approximately 4 hours.

When the eggplant is tender, (3 1/2 - 4 1/2 hours), stir to combine the mix.

 Combine sugar and vinegar and add to the slow cooker with the capers and basil.

Stir well, cover and cook 10-15 minutes, to blend the flavors.

Serve over couscous or polenta and garnish with feta cheese.

Variation: Add a can of garbanzo beans, putting them in the slow cooker first.

Nutritional Facts:

Serving Size: 1 (438 g)

Servings Per Recipe: 4

Amount Per Serving:

Calories: 166.1	Sodium: 365.1 mg
Calories from Fat: 28	Carbs: 32.7 g
Total Fat: 3.2 g	Fiber: 11.4 g
Sat. Fat: 0.5 g	Sugars: 19.6 g
Cholesterol: 0.0 mg	Protein: 6.6 g

Slow Cooker Rotisserie Style Chicken

Total Time: 2 hrs. 15 mins.

Prep Time: 15 mins.

Cook Time: 2 hrs.

Serves: 4

Save money by cooking your own Rotisserie chicken at home with this easy slow cooker method. Cooking at home also allows you to know the freshness and quality of the food you eat. Cook one of these and have chicken on hand for sandwiches or adding to salads.

Ingredients:

1 Tablespoon salt

2 teaspoons paprika

2 teaspoons dried oregano leaves

2 teaspoons dried thyme leaves

1/2 teaspoon dried rosemary leaves

1 teaspoon freshly ground black pepper

1 teaspoon garlic powder

1(3 lbs.) roasting chicken

1 cup onion, roughly chopped

1 lemon, cut in half

Directions:

Wash chicken well under cold water. Remove bag in cavity. Discard or save for another use. Dry well with paper towels.

In a small bowl, combine all ingredients except chicken, onion and lemon.

Rub herb mixture inside and outside of chicken.

Place in a pan and cover well with plastic wrap.

Refrigerate overnight.

Remove chicken from fridge and stuff onion and lemon halves into cavity.

Place in crockpot on Low for 6-8 hours or High for 2-4 hours. Chicken is done when juices run clear and internal temperature should reach 165 degrees.

Let stand 15 minutes before carving.

Variation: substitute 4 bone in, skin on, chicken breasts for whole chicken. Place some sliced onion in the bottom of the slow cooker, top with chicken and add onion slices and lemon slices on top.

Nutritional Facts:

Serving Size: 1 (268 g)

Servings Per Recipe: 4

Amount Per Serving:

Calories: 500.7	Sodium: 1896.7 mg
Calories from Fat: 315	Carbs: 6.0 g
Total Fat: 35.0 g	Fiber 1.7 g
Sat. Fat:10.0 g	Sugars: 1.8 g
Cholesterol: 160.4 mg	Protein: 38.5 g

Chicken with 40 Cloves of Garlic Slow Cooker Style

Total Time: 8 hrs. 15 mins.

Prep Time: 15 mins

Cook Time: 8 hrs.

Servings: 4

This might seem like a lot of garlic but the garlic roasts and turns into a rich, buttery spread which is delicious on crusty French bread or tomatoes, sliced or cherry. If you're making a salad to accompany this dish, try adding some of the roasted garlic to your salad dressing.

Ingredients:

2 sprigs fresh thyme

2 sprigs fresh rosemary

2 sprigs fresh sage

2 sprigs fresh Italian parsley

1 cup chicken broth

40 cloves garlic, unpeeled

1 teaspoon kosher salt

1/4 teaspoon ground black pepper

1(4 lbs.) whole chicken

2 stalks celery, sliced

1 loaf French bread, sliced

Directions:

Remove bag of chicken parts from cavity. Reserve for another use or discard. Wash chicken well under cold water. Set aside to drain.

Place 1 sprig thyme, rosemary, sage and parsley in chicken cavity.

Place celery in crock pot.

Put chicken on top of celery.

Pour chicken stock around the chicken.

Scatter garlic around chicken.

Chop remaining herbs. Sprinkle herbs, salt and pepper over chicken.

Cover cook on Low 8- 10 hours or on High 4- 6 hours.

To serve, place chicken, garlic and celery on serving platter.

Squeeze roasted garlic out of skins and spread on toasted French bread slices.

Nutritional Facts:

Serving Size: 1 (662 g)

Servings Per Recipe: 4

Amount Per Serving:

Calories: 741	Sodium: 1070mg
Calories from Fat: 128	Carbs: 10.5g
Total Fat: 14.2g	Fiber: 0.8g
Sat. Fat: 4.0g	Sugars: 0.6g
Cholesterol: 349mg	Protein: 134.6g

Lemon Chicken with Broccoli

Total Time: 3 hours, 20 minutes

Prep Time: 20 minutes

Cook Time: 3 hours

Serves: 4

Ingredients

1 to 1 1/2 lbs. boneless chicken breast strips

2 Tablespoons dry seasoning mix (recipe below)

Dash cayenne pepper

2 Tablespoons all-purpose flour

1 large zip top bag

1 Tablespoon extra virgin olive oil

2 large lemons, juiced (should yield 1/2 cup of juice)

1/2 cup chicken broth

2 big broccoli crowns cut into spears

Or substitute asparagus, green beans, carrots, zucchini, just about anything that appeals to you.

An excellent combination of vegetables for this dish is a can of artichoke hearts, quartered; some jarred roasted peppers and a sprinkling of feta cheese as its being served.

Zest of 1 lemon, garnish. Hint: zest your lemon before you juice it.

Directions:

Wash chicken well snipping away any pieces of fat. Dry with paper towels.

Put seasoning mix, cayenne pepper and flour in the zip top bag. Add the chicken and shake to coat.

In a large sauté pan heat olive oil to hot but not smoking, add chicken and cook until browned on both sides, about 10 minutes. Do this in batches if you need to.

Pour the lemon juice and chicken broth into the slow cooker.

Add Chicken.

Cover and cook on high for 2 hours, then add the broccoli.

Cook for 1 hour, or until broccoli is tender.

Plate chicken and drizzle lemon sauce from bottom of slow cooker over the chicken and the broccoli when serving.

Serve with brown rice.

Garnish with lemon zest.

Nutritional Facts:

Serving: 295g

Servings Per Recipe: 4

Amount Per Serving:

Calories: 311	Trans Fat: 0 g	Fiber: 3.2 g
Calories from Fat: 115	Cholesterol: 101mg	Sugars: 2.7
Total Fat: 12.8 g	Sodium: 237 mg	Protein: 37.3 g
Sat. Fat: 3.1g	Carbs: 11.2 g	

All Purpose Seasoning Mix

Total Time: 5 mins.

Prep Time: 5 mins.

Cook Time: 0 mins.

Serves: 24

Yield: 8 Tbsp.

This is a delicious all-purpose dry seasoning mix which will keep in a tightly covered container for up to 6 months. It's a versatile mix which can be used in cooking dishes such as spaghetti sauce, soups, stews, etc. It makes a delicious salad dressing, marinade or garlic bread too!

Ingredients:

1 1/2 teaspoons garlic powder

1 Tablespoon onion powder

2 Tablespoons oregano, ground or whole leaves

1 Tablespoon dried parsley

2 Tablespoons salt or 2 Tablespoons salt substitute (optional)

1 teaspoon freshly ground black pepper

1 teaspoon basil, ground or whole leaves

1/4 teaspoon thyme, ground or whole leaves

1/2 teaspoon dried celery leaves or dried celery flakes

Directions:

Mix all ingredients together in an air-tight container. Cover tightly and store in a cool dry place.

To use for Italian Salad Dressing or Marinade: Combine 2 Tablespoons of this mix with 1/4 cup red or white wine vinegar, 2 Tablespoons water, and 1/2 to 2/3 cup extra virgin olive oil.

Shake before using.

Super Easy Chicken Cacciatore

Total Time: 8 hrs. 10 mins.

Prep Time: 10 mins.

Cook Time: 8 hrs.

Servings: 4-6

Ingredients:

7-8 boneless, skinless chicken thighs

1 (15 oz.) can diced tomatoes

1 (6 oz.) can tomato paste

1 (14 1/2 ounce) can tomato sauce

1 onion, roughly chopped

2 green bell peppers, seeded cut into 1/2" squares

8 oz. fresh mushrooms, sliced

1 bay leaf

1 teaspoon kosher salt

1/2 teaspoon freshly ground black pepper

2 cloves garlic, minced

1/2 teaspoon thyme

2 teaspoons Italian seasoning

Parmesan cheese, for garnish

Directions:

Wash chicken thighs well and snip away unwanted fat.

Add all ingredients to crock pot, mix well, making sure chicken is covered.

Cover, cook on low heat 7 to 9 hours or high heat for about 3 to 4 hours.

Serve over polenta, couscous or pasta. For a delicious change try mashed potatoes.

Pass Parmesan cheese at the table.

Serve with a green salad.

Nutritional Facts:

Serving Size: 1 (287 g)

Servings Per Recipe: 4

Amount Per Serving:

Calories 268.6	Sodium: 1699.1 mg
Calories from Fat: 65	Carbs: 24.7 g
Total Fat: 7.2 g	Fiber: 5.7 g
Sat. Fat: 1.5 g	Sugars: 16.7 g
Cholesterol: 100.2 mg	Protein: 29.2 g

Mediterranean Chicken with Wine and Olives

Total Time: 5 hrs. 15 mins.

Prep Time: 15 mins.

Cook Time: 5 hrs.

Servings: 6-8

Ingredients:

1 medium onion, cut in wedges

1 green bell pepper, cut in strips

4 cloves garlic, roughly chopped

42 1/2 ozs. (1- 28oz. can & 14.5 oz. can) stewed tomatoes

6 ozs. tomato paste

1 cup dry red wine or 1 cup dry white wine

4 -6 boneless, skinless chicken breasts

1/4 cup fresh flat leaf parsley, chopped

2 Tablespoons lemon juice

1/2 teaspoon nutmeg

Kosher salt, to taste

Freshly ground black pepper

1 Tablespoon dried basil

6 ozs. Kalamata olives, pitted

1 Tablespoon crushed red pepper flakes, or more or less to taste

Directions:

Wash chicken pieces well with cold water and snip away any unwanted fat.

Mix all ingredients together in slow cooker, making sure chicken pieces are covered.

Cook on High for 5 hours or Low for 8 hours. Make sure chicken is fully cooked. Chicken is cooked when the juices run clear or if you have a thermometer it should read at least 165°.

Serve over cooked spaghetti squash or polenta. Sprinkle with parmesan cheese.

How To Cook Spaghetti Squash:
The easiest way to cook spaghetti squash is to cut it lengthwise. You don't want to cut it up too small unless you want short strands. Scrape out the seeds and pulp as you would with any squash or pumpkin and remove seeds. Place it on a baking sheet rind sides up. Bake at 375° for 45 minutes. Remove from skin with fork and toss with extra virgin olive oil, salt and pepper.

Nutritional Facts:

Serving Size: 1 (330 g)

Servings Per Recipe: 6

Amount Per Serving:

Calories: 252.8	Sodium: 1009.1 mg
Calories from Fat: 52	Carbs: 25.5 g
Total Fat: 5.7 g	Fiber: 5.0 g
Sat. Fat: 1.0 g	Sugars: 12.8 g
Cholesterol: 50.3 mg	Protein: 20.7 g

Greek Chicken and Vegetable Casserole

Total Time: 4 hrs. 30 mins.

Prep Time: 30 mins.

Cook Time: 4 hrs.

Servings: 3-4

Ingredients:

6 chicken thighs

1 Tablespoon extra virgin olive oil

1 teaspoon kosher salt

1 teaspoon freshly ground black pepper

1 large onion, coarsely chopped

1 1/2 cups fresh mushrooms, cut in thick slices

2 small zucchini, squash, cut into 1 inch chunks

1 (15 ounce) can chickpeas or other white beans, drained and rinsed

1 (15 ounce) can diced tomatoes

1 cup Kalamata olives, pitted

1/2 cup sun-dried tomatoes, chopped

2 teaspoons fresh lemon juice

1 teaspoon Greek seasoning (such as Cavender's)

3 cloves garlic, minced

2 Tablespoons capers

Directions:

Wash chicken pieces well with cold water and snip away any unwanted fat. Dry with paper towels.

Season chicken with salt and pepper.

Heat olive oil in a large sauté pan over medium-high heat until hot but not smoking. Add chicken and brown on both sides. Remove from heat and set aside.

Place onion, zucchini, and mushrooms in the bottom of the slow cooker. Place chicken on top of the vegetables. Spread chickpeas over the chicken.

Combine tomatoes, olives, sundried tomatoes, garlic, lemon juice, and Greek seasoning in a small bowl, pour over chicken.

Sprinkle capers on top of the mixture in the slow cooker.

Cover and cook on High for 4 hours or Low for 6-8 until juices run clear or thermometer registers 165°F.

Serve with a big green salad.

Nutritional Facts:

Serving Size: 1 (538 g)

Calories from Fat 386

Servings Per Recipe: 3

Amount Per Serving:	Sodium: 1907.8 mg
Calories: 771.6	Total Carbs: 55.1 g
Total Fat: 42.9 g	Fiber: 13.0 g
Sat. Fat: 9.9 g	Sugars: 8.6 g
Cholesterol: 157.9 mg	Protein: 45.0 g

Herbed Chicken Breasts with White Beans

Total Time: 4-8 hrs. 20 mins.

Prep Time: 20 mins

Cook Time: 4 -8 hrs.

Servings: 6

Ingredients:

2 Tablespoons extra virgin olive oil

4-6 boneless, skinless chicken breasts

1 cup carrot, sliced

1/2 cup celery, sliced

1 (16 ounce) can great northern beans, drained and rinsed

1/2 teaspoon salt

1/2 teaspoon freshly ground black pepper

1 teaspoon dried rosemary

1/2 teaspoon dried thyme

1/3 cup fat-free Italian salad dressing

Directions:

Wash chicken pieces well with cold water, snipping away any unwanted fat. Dry with paper towels.

In medium sauté pan, heat olive oil until hot but not smoking. Add chicken breasts and cook until well browned. Remove from pan and drain.

Place carrots, celery, and beans in slow cooker. Top with chicken breasts.

Combine salt, pepper, rosemary, and Italian dressing and pour over ingredients in slow cooker. Stir slightly to combine.

Cover and cook on Low for 8-9 hours or on High for 4-5 hours.

Nutritional Facts:

Serving Size: 1 (185 g)

Servings Per Recipe: 6

Amount Per Serving:

Calories: 211.7	Sodium: 410.4 mg
Calories from Fat: 53	Carbs.: 15.8 g
Total Fat: 5.9 g	Fiber: 4.9 g
Sat. Fat:1.0 g	Sugars: 2.1 g
Cholesterol: 45.8 mg	Protein: 23.4 g

Peru com Porto, Frutas e Azeitonas

Total Time: 6 hrs. 10 mins.

Prep Time: 10 mins.

Cook Time: 6 hrs.

Servings: 8

A delectable Portuguese twist on turkey.

Substitute a cut up chicken if you can't find turkey thighs.

Ingredients:

1 cup thinly sliced leek

1 cup ruby port or 1 cup other sweet red wine

3/4 cup dried cherries

3/4 cup pitted Kalamata olive

1/3 cup fresh orange juice

1 teaspoon paprika

1 teaspoon crushed red pepper flakes

4 fresh thyme sprigs

1 (3 inch) cinnamon stick

1 1/2 teaspoons kosher salt, divided

3 1/2 lbs. turkey thighs, skinned

1 tablespoon ground cumin

Directions:

In a slow cooker combine thinly sliced leek, ruby port, dried cherries, Kalamata olives, fresh orange juice, paprika, crushed red pepper flakes, thyme sprigs, and cinnamon stick, stirring to combine. Stir in 1/2 teaspoon salt.

Wash turkey with cold water, snipping away excess fat. Dry with paper towels.

Sprinkle with remaining 1 teaspoon salt and cumin.

Place in slow cooker. Cover with lid, and cook on Low 6 hours.

Remove cinnamon stick and discard

Serve with couscous or polenta.

Nutritional Facts:

Serving Size: 1 (66 g)

Servings Per Recipe: 8

Amount Per Serving:

Calories: 567	Sodium: 926mg
Calories from Fat: 139	Carbs: 17.0g
Total Fat: 15.4g	Fiber: 1.4g
Sat. Fat: 4.6g	Sugars: 2.1g
Cholesterol: 200mg	Protein: 78.4g

Vermont Style Sweet and Tangy Turkey Thighs

Total Time: 3 hrs. 20 mins.

Prep Time: 20 mins.

Cook Time: 3 hrs.

Servings: 4

Ingredients:

1 lb. new red potatoes, quartered

4 carrots, peeled and cut in chunks

2 -2 1/2 lbs. skinless turkey thighs

1/3 cup coarse grain brown mustard

1/3 cup pure maple syrup

1 Tablespoon quick-cooking tapioca

Directions:

Wash turkey well with cold water, snipping away any excess fat.

Place potatoes and carrots in the bottom of the slow cooker. Place turkey thighs on top.

In a small bowl, stir together mustard, syrup and tapioca. Pour over turkey. Cover, cook on low for 6-7 hours or on high for 3-3 1/2 hours.

Nutritional Facts:

Serving Size: 1 (371 g)

Servings Per Recipe: 4

Amount Per Serving:

Calories: 172.1	**Sodium: 31.4 mg**
Calories from Fat: 1	Carbs: 41.6 g
Total Fat: 0.1 g	Fiber: 2.5 g
Sat. Fat: 0.0 g	Sugars: 19.6 g
Cholesterol: 0.0 mg	Protein: 2.3 g

Greek Style Turkey Breast

Total Time: 7 hrs. 20 mins.

Prep Time: 20 mins.

Cook Time: 7 hrs.

Servings: 8

Ingredients:

2 cups (about 1 large) onions, chopped

1/4 cup Greek black olives, pitted

1/4 cup Greek green olives, pitted

1/2 cup oil-packed dried tomatoes, thinly sliced

2 Tablespoons fresh lemon juice

1 teaspoon all-purpose Greek seasoning (such as Cavender's)

1/2 teaspoon kosher salt

1/4 teaspoon freshly ground black pepper

1 (4 lb.) boneless turkey breast, trimmed

1/2 cup chicken broth, divided

3 tablespoons all-purpose flour

Directions:

Wash turkey well with cold water, snipping away any excess fat.

Combine onions, Greek black olives, Greek green olives, dried tomatoes, fresh lemon juice, Greek seasoning, salt, pepper, and turkey breast in slow cooker. Add 1/4 cup broth. Cover and cook on Low for 7 hours.

Combine remaining 1/4 cup broth and flour in small bowl, stir with a whisk until smooth.

Add broth mixture to slow cooker.

Cover and cook on Low for 30 minutes.

Remove turkey breast from slow cooker and allow to sit 15 minutes before slicing.

Slice turkey and serve with sauce.

Nutritional Facts:

Serving Size: 1 (301 g)

Servings Per Recipe: 8

Amount Per Serving:	Sodium 460.1 mg
Calories: 404.7	Carbs. 8.7 g
Calories from Fat: 153	Fiber 1.5 g
Total Fat: 17.1 g	Sugars 3.1 g
Cholesterol: 147.5 mg	Protein 51.3 g

All Purpose Greek Seasoning Blend

Total Time: 5 mins

Prep Time: 5 mins

Cook Time: **0 mins**

Yield: 1/4 cup

Ingredients:

2 teaspoons dried oregano

2 teaspoons salt

1 1/2 teaspoons onion powder

1 1/2 teaspoons garlic powder

1 teaspoon cornstarch

1 teaspoon freshly ground black pepper

1 teaspoon dried parsley flakes

1 teaspoon paprika

1/2 teaspoon ground cinnamon

1/2 teaspoon ground nutmeg

1/2 teaspoon thyme

1/2 teaspoon dried mint, optional

Directions:

Combine all ingredients.

Store in an airtight container.

This has many uses. It makes a nice salad dressing, is also good on roasted vegetables, poultry, fish, red meat, or pork.

Turkey Breast White Beans and Artichokes

Total Time: 7 hrs. 5 mins.

Prep Time: 5 mins.

Cook Time: 7 hrs.

Servings: 8

Ingredients:

2 (15 oz.) cans cannellini beans, rinsed and drained

1 (14 1/2 oz.) can diced tomatoes, undrained

1 (14 oz.) can quartered artichokes, drained

1 small onion, chopped

3 cloves garlic, minced

2 lbs. boneless, skinless turkey breasts

1 teaspoon dried sage

1 teaspoon dried rosemary

1/2 teaspoon dried thyme

1 teaspoon freshly ground black pepper

1 teaspoon kosher salt

1 1/2 cups dry white wine

Directions:

Wash turkey well with cold water, snipping away any excess fat.

Place beans, tomatoes with their juice, artichokes, onion and garlic in slow cooker.

Lay turkey breasts on top.

Sprinkle with sage, rosemary, thyme, pepper and salt.

Pour white wine over top.

Cover and cook on Low for 5-7 hours.

Nutritional Facts:

Serving Size: 1 (379 g)

Servings Per Recipe: 8

Amount Per Serving:

Calories: 355.6	Sodium: 437.6 mg
Calories from Fat: 11	Carbs: 38.2 g
Total Fat: 1.3 g	Fiber: 10.4 g
Sat. Fat: 0.3 g	Sugars: 3.2 g
Cholesterol: 70.3 mg	Protein: 40.5 g

Beef:

Mediterranean Pot Roast in Red Wine Sauce
Total Time: 6 hrs. 10 mins.

Prep Time: 10 mins.

Cook Time: 6 hrs.

Servings: 8-10

Ingredients:

1 Tablespoon extra virgin olive oil

3 lbs. boneless beef chuck roast

1 teaspoon kosher salt

1 teaspoon dried oregano

1 teaspoon dried basil

1/2 teaspoon dried rosemary

1/2 teaspoon dried thyme

2 large cloves garlic, minced

1/3 cup dried tomatoes packed in oil, drained and chopped

1/2 cup sliced Kalamata olives

2 cups red wine

1/2 cup frozen pearl onions

2 Tablespoons cornstarch

2 Tablespoons cold water

Directions:

Wash beef well under cold water. Dry with paper towels.

In a large sauté pan, heat olive oil until hot but not smoking.

Add beef to pan and cook until well browned on all sides, about 10 minutes.

Sprinkle with salt, Italian seasoning and garlic; remove from skillet.

Place beef, seasoned side up in slow cooker.

Spread tomatoes and olives over roast.

Add wine and onions.

Cover and cook on low 5-6 hours till beef is tender.

Remove beef from slow cooker; cover and let stand 15 minutes.

Meanwhile, place cornstarch in a small dish or measuring cup. Add water, stir to combine, whisk into slow cooker, cover and cook until thickened.

Slice beef; serve with beef juice and vegetables from slow cooker.

Nutritional Facts:

Serving Size: 1 (159 g)

Servings Per Recipe: 8

Amount Per Serving:

Calories: 454.6	Sodium: 512.3 mg
Calories from Fat: 313	Carbs: 1.7 g
Total Fat: 34.8 g	Fiber: 0.5 g
Sat. Fat: 13.6 g	Sugars: 0.0 g
Cholesterol: 117.4 mg	Protein: 31.7 g

Mediterranean Pot Roast with Vegetables

Total Time: 10 hrs. 15 mins.

Prep Time: 15 mins.

Cook Time: 10 hrs.

Yield: 4 to 6 servings

Ingredients:

3 1/2 lbs. beef chuck roast

8 new red potatoes

1/2 lb. baby carrots

8 oz. whole mushroom caps, cleaned, stems trimmed

6 cloves garlic, peeled, whole

1 teaspoon kosher salt

1 teaspoon dried rosemary, crushed

1/2 teaspoon dried thyme

1/2 teaspoon freshly ground black pepper

1/4 cup water

1/4 cup dry red wine

2 Tablespoons cornstarch

2 Tablespoons water

Chopped parsley

Directions:

Wash beef well under cold water, trimming fat as needed.

Place potatoes, carrots, mushrooms and garlic in slow cooker.

Rub beef with rosemary, thyme, salt and pepper.

Place on top of vegetables. Add water and wine.

Cover and cook on Low 10 to 11 hours or until beef and vegetables are tender.

Remove pot roast; trim fat if necessary. Arrange pot roast and vegetables on serving platter. Cover and keep warm.

Just before serving, carve port roast across the grain into thin slices.

To make gravy, strain cooking liquid; skim off fat, and transfer 2 cups of cooking liquid to a small saucepan. Place cornstarch in a small dish or measuring cup and add cold water. Stir to dissolve. Whisk into cooking liquid. Cook and stir 1 minute or until thickened.

Garnish beef and vegetables with parsley; serve with gravy.

Nutritional Facts:

Serving Size: 1 (3702 g)

Servings Per Recipe: 4

Serving Size 617 g

Amount Per Serving:

Calories: 1,195	Sodium: 605mg
Calories from Fat: 667	Carbs.: 51.9g
Total Fat: 74.1g	Fiber: 6.1g
Sat. Fat: 29.4g	Sugars: 4.7g
Cholesterol: 273mg	Protein: 75.0g

Moroccan Beef Tagine

Total Time: 6-10 hrs. 15 mins.

Prep Time: 15 mins.

Cook Time: 6-10 hrs.

Serves: 6-8

Ingredients:

3 lbs, stewing beef, trimmed of fat & cubed

1 Tablespoon extra virgin olive oil

1 lb, onion, cut in quarters

4 -6 cloves garlic, minced

1 lb. carrot, peeled and cut into chunks

1 cup diced tomatoes with juice

4 oz. dates, pitted

6 oz. prunes, pitted

2 Tablespoons honey

2 cups beef stock

1 cinnamon stick

6 teaspoons Ras El Hanout Spice Mix (see recipe below)

Kosher salt, to taste

Freshly ground black pepper

2 oz. sliced almonds, toasted

2 Tablespoons fresh cilantro, chopped

Directions:

Wash stewing beef under cold water, dry with paper towels.

Bring a saucepan of water to a boil, drop in the carrots and cook for about 3-5 minutes. Drain, rinse in cold water. Set aside.

Preheat slow cooker to High.

In a large sauté pan, heat half the olive oil until hot but not smoking. Add the onion quarters and quickly brown until charred and well colored. Transfer to the slow cooker.

Add the garlic and carrots to the onions in the slow cooker.

Stir together the stock, honey and all spices. Add to the slow cooker and mix well.

Add the cinnamon stick, tomatoes, dates and prunes to the slow cooker and mix well.

Heat the remaining olive oil in the sauté pan and brown the beef cubes in small batches to sear and seal them. As beef is browned, add to slow cooker.

When all the beef has been added, give it a stir and season with salt and pepper.

Cook on High for 6-10 hours, depending on your slow cooker.

Remove cinnamon stick and serve.

Serve with couscous and garnish with the chopped fresh cilantro and sliced almonds.

Nutrition Facts:

Serving Size 517 g

Amount Per Serving:

Calories: 656	Trans Fat: 0.0g	Fiber: 7.7g
Calories from Fat: 153	Cholesterol: 203mg	Sugars: 36.2g
Total Fat: 17.0g	Sodium:335mg	Protein: 72.2g
Sat. Fat: 5.8g	Carbs: 53.8g	

Ras El Hanout

Ras El Hanout is a North African Spice whose name, when roughly translated means "House Blend." Its literal translation from Arabic is "head of the shop," implying that it's "the best (or top) of the shop. It can contain as many as 50 ingredients including rosebuds and Spanish fly. Every Moroccan shop keeper has his own secret blend of herbs and spices.

While some Moroccans use it in daily cooking, others reserve it for specialty dishes. It's used to season many things from beef and pork to eggs.

Ras El Hanout is a fantastic blend of spices and is very versatile. Try mixing it with some yogurt, coat chicken and then broil, roast or grill. It's also delicious as a rub for grilled salmon.

Ingredients:

1 teaspoon ground cumin

1 teaspoon ground ginger

1 teaspoon turmeric

1 teaspoon kosher salt

3/4 teaspoon sugar

3/4 teaspoon fresh ground black pepper

1/2 teaspoon cinnamon

1/2 teaspoon ground coriander

1/2 teaspoon cayenne

1/2 teaspoon ground allspice

1/2 teaspoon ground fennel

1/4 teaspoon ground cloves

Directions:

Mix together, and store in an airtight container.

Yield: 1/2 cup

Greek Beef and Eggplant

Total Time: 8-10 hrs. 25 mins.

Prep Time: 15 mins.

Cook Time: 8-10 hrs. 10 mins.

Servings: 6-8

Ingredients:

2 lbs. lean stewing beef, cut in 1 1/2" chunks

2 medium onions, sliced thin

2 red, yellow and/or orange bell pepper, cut in strips

2 cloves garlic, minced

1/4 cup extra virgin olive oil

8 Japanese eggplants (the long, thin, striated purple & white ones)

1 cup beef stock

1 (16 oz.) can tomato sauce

1 Tablespoon red wine vinegar

3/4 teaspoon sugar

1/2 teaspoon cinnamon

1/8 teaspoon allspice

1/8 teaspoon ground cloves

Kosher salt, to taste

Freshly ground black pepper, to taste

1/4 cup minced parsley

1/2 cup cubed feta cheese as garnish, optional

Directions

Wash beef, trim away any excess fat and dry with paper towels.

Wash the eggplant, trim top and bottom.

Slice unpeeled eggplant into 1" thick slices.

Heat 2 Tbsp. olive oil in a large skillet, brown the beef, onions, peppers, garlic and eggplant until dark golden-brown, adding more oil as necessary. Drain.

Place in slow cooker.

Combine the beef stock, tomato sauce, vinegar, sugar, spices, salt and pepper to taste. Stir into meat.

Cover and cook on low heat for 8-10 hours.

If serving with pasta, prepare pasta until al dente, pour onto a large serving platter and cover with meat, eggplant and sauce.

Garnish with parsley and feta and serve.

Accompany this with a big green salad, lots of crusty bread for mopping the sauce, and plenty of red wine.

Nutritional Facts:

Serving Size: 1 (797 g)

Servings Per Recipe: 6

Amount Per Serving:

Calories 587.0	Sodium 648.3 mg
Calories from Fat 253	Carbs. 50.4 g
Total Fat 28.1 g	Fiber 26.8 g
Sat. Fat 8.4 g	Sugars 22.5 g
Cholesterol 110.5 mg	Protein 40.7 g

Mediterranean Beef Stew with Olives and Sun-Dried Tomatoes

Total Time: 8-9 hrs. 25 mins.

Prep Time: 25 mins.

Cook Time: 8-9 hrs.

Servings: 6-8

Ingredients:

2 lbs. lean stewing beef, such as bottom round, cut into 1-1/2 inch cubes

2 Tablespoons extra virgin olive oil

2 medium onions, sliced

3 garlic cloves, thinly sliced

3/4 cup dry vermouth or dry white wine

1 (28 ounce) can San Marzano tomatoes, undrained

1 1/2 cups beef stock

2 teaspoons balsamic vinegar

1/4 teaspoon freshly ground black pepper

1/8 teaspoon crushed red pepper flakes

1/3 cup Kalamata olives, pitted and cut in half

1/2 cup sun-dried tomatoes packed in oil, drained and chopped

1/2 cup lightly packed fresh basil, shredded

Directions:

Wash beef under cold water and dry with paper towels.

In a large sauté pan, heat the olive oil over moderately high heat until hot but not smoking. Add the meat in 2 batches and cook, turning, until nicely browned, about 5 minutes per batch. Transfer meat to slow cooker.

Add the onions to the sauté pan and cook, stirring occasionally, until golden and beginning to brown around the edges, about 5 minutes.

Add the garlic and cook until softened and fragrant, about 1 minute.

Pour in the vermouth and boil until reduced by half, 1 to 2 minutes.

"Smoosh" the tomatoes with your fingers, breaking them into small pieces. Add to slow cooker along with their juice, vinegar, black pepper, hot pepper, and stock.

Cover slow cooker, set to Low and cook 8-9 hours. Add the olives and sun dried tomatoes and cook 1 hour longer, or until the beef is tender.

(This can be made up to this point up to 2 days in advance.)

Just before serving, stir in the fresh basil.

Serve with couscous, polenta or rice.

Nutritional Facts:

Serving Size: 1 (279 g)

Servings Per Recipe: 6

Amount Per Serving:

Calories: 414.7	Sodium: 12.9 mg
Calories from Fat: 208	Carbs: 12.4 g
Total Fat: 23.2 g	Fiber: 2.9 g
Sat. Fat: 7.6 g	Sugars: 6.6 g
Cholesterol: 110.5 mg	Protein: 33.6 g

Pork:

Tuscan Pork and White Beans
Total Time: 16 hrs. 20 mins.

Prep Time: 20 mins.

Cook Time: 16 hrs.

Serves: 8

No one herb in this recipe jumps out at you but instead they all work together to add so much to the dish. It smells so good in the slow cooker on a cold, snowy day. It's like French comfort food.

Ingredients:

2 cups dried Great Northern beans, or other small white beans

1 Tablespoon fresh sage, minced

2 teaspoons kosher salt

1 teaspoon ground fennel seed

8 cloves garlic, minced

2 1/2 lbs. boneless pork shoulder, trimmed

3 cups chicken stock

1 cup dry white wine

2 bay leaves

Directions:

Pick over and wash beans removing any seeds or debris. Place in a large bowl. Cover with a generous amount of water, up to 2 inches above beans. Cover and let stand overnight.

Wash pork under cold water and dry with paper towels.

Combine sage, fennel. garlic and salt until it forms a rough paste. Rub it over the outside of the pork. Place pork in a glass baking dish or other non-reactive pan, cover with plastic wrap and refrigerate overnight.

Next morning, heat a large sauté pan. Add pork and brown on all sides. This will take about 10 minutes. When browned, transfer to slow cooker.

Add chicken broth to sauté pan and stir, scraping any brown bits off the bottom. Bring to a boil, add the wine and boil for 3 minutes. Add to slow cooker.

Drain beans and add to slow cooker along with bay leaves.

Cover. Cook on High for 8 hours. If your slow cooker runs hot, start this on High, and reduce it to Low after 3 hours, or if the of the slow cooker contents begin to boil, reduce it to Low.

Nutritional Facts:

Serving Size: 1 (317 g)

Servings Per Recipe: 8

Amount Per Serving:

Calories: 540.3	Sodium: 538.2 mg
Calories from Fat: 265	Carbs: 32.8 g
Total Fat: 29.5 g	Fiber :12.9 g
Sat. Fat: 10.0 g	Sugars: 2.0 g
Cholesterol: 100.7 mg	Protein: 35.5 g

:

Pork Mediterranean Style

Total Time: 24 hrs. 30 mins.

Prep Time: 30 mins.

Cook Time: 24 hrs.

Serves: 6-8

This is such a flexible recipe. You can use boneless pork loin if the pork shoulders in your market are too big to fit in your slow cooker. I bought two1 1/2 pound pork loins. The meat fell apart easily after 7 - 8 hours.

It's also flexible in the way you can use it. For example, use it as a gyro by stuffing stuffed it in a pita and topping with plain yogurt, cucumber and feta.

Combine it with BBQ sauce and serve with a side of coleslaw and a pickle.

Use it in a "Cuban Wrap" by placing the shredded pork down the middle of a flour tortilla, top it with sliced Swiss cheese and sliced pickle. Pop it in the microwave and roll it up.

Ingredients:

1 (3 lb.) boneless pork shoulder

2 teaspoons dried oregano

For the marinade:

1/4 cup extra virgin olive oil

1/4 cup fresh lemon juice

1 teaspoon dried oregano

2 teaspoons dried mint

2 teaspoons Dijon mustard

2 teaspoons pesto sauce

6 cloves garlic, crushed

Salt and freshly ground black pepper

Directions:

Wash pork under cold water, dry with paper towels and poke it all over with a sharp knife creating 1/2" deep or slightly deeper slits.

Rub it all over with the oregano and as you do, try to get it in the slits.

Place roast in a glass baking pan or other non-reactive pan. Cover with plastic wrap and refrigerate for an hour or overnight.

Mix all the ingredients for the marinade.

Pour over, rubbing in half of marinade.

Flip pork over and repeat, cover and refrigerate for 10-12 hours.

When ready to cook, bring roast back to room temperature.

Preheat a large frying pan or skillet on the top of the stove.

Scrape off as much marinade as possible and place that, together with the remaining marinade in your slow cooker and turn it to Low.

When skillet is hot, brown the roast on all sides. This will take about 10 minutes.

Remove pork to slow cooker and add 1/4 cup water to the sauté pan, bring to boil scraping up all the small, browned bits.

Add pan juices to slow cooker, cover and cook on low for 8-10 hours.

Optional: Add 2 Tablespoons of heavy cream to juices or serve as they are.

Note: if using as a shredded filling to serve in pita, cook the pork 1-2 hours longer and shred it using 2 forks.

Nutritional Facts:

Serving Size: 1 (188 g)

Servings Per Recipe: 6

Amount Per Serving:

Calories: 663.4	Sodium: 174.4 mg
Calories from Fat: 494	Carbs: 2.3 g
Total Fat: 54.9 g	Fiber: 0.3 g
Sat. Fat: 17.1 g	Sugars: 0.3 g
Cholesterol: 161.1 mg	Protein: 38.2 g

Easy White Bean Cassoulet

Total Time: 8 hrs. 20 mins.

Prep Time: 20 mins.

Cook Time: 8 hrs.

Servings: 6

This isn't a traditional Cassoulet by any stretch of the imagination but it is hearty comfort food for busy cooks!

Ingredients:

1 Tablespoon extra virgin olive oil

1 1/2 cups onions, chopped

1 1/2 cups carrots, peeled and diced about the same size as your beans

1 cup parsnip, peeled and diced about the same size as your beans

2 stalks celery, chopped

2 cloves garlic, minced

2 (16 ounce) cans white beans, rinsed & drained

3/4 cup vegetable stock

1/2 teaspoon dried thyme

1/4 teaspoon kosher salt

1/4 teaspoon freshly ground black pepper

1 (28 ounce) can diced tomatoes, undrained

1 bay leaf

1/4 cup dry breadcrumbs

1/4 cup fresh Parmesan cheese, grated

2 Tablespoons extra virgin olive oil

8 oz. Italian sausage, chopped

2 Tablespoons fresh parsley

Directions:

In a large sauté pan, heat olive oil over medium heat until hot but not smoking.

Add onion, carrots, parsnips, celery, and garlic. Cover and cook 5 minutes; stirring occasionally.

Place cooked vegetables in slow cooker. Add beans, vegetable stock, thyme, salt, pepper, tomatoes, and bay leaf.

Cover and cook on Low 8 hours or until vegetables are tender. Remove Bay leaf.

Sauté sausage until browned. Drain off fat.

Combine breadcrumbs, parmesan cheese and olive oil in a small bowl; toss with a fork until moistened. Stir breadcrumb mixture and cooked sausage into bean mixture.

Cover and cook 30 minutes, or until heated through.

Sprinkle with parsley.

Nutritional Facts:

Serving Size: 1 (472 g)

Servings Per Recipe: 6

Amount Per Serving:

Calories: 494.3	Sodium: 553.7 mg
Calories from Fat: 154	Carbs: 55.1 g
Total Fat: 29.1 g	Fiber: 11.9 g
Sat. Fat 11.0 g	Sugars: 9.1 g
Cholesterol: 17.9 mg	Protein: 18.9 g

Orange Pork Roast

Total Time: 10 hrs. 15 mins.

Prep Time: 15 mins.

Cook Time: 10 hrs.

Servings: 8

Ingredients:

2 1/2-3 lbs. pork sirloin roast

1 teaspoon dried oregano, crushed

1/2 teaspoon ground ginger

1/2 teaspoon freshly ground black pepper

2 Tablespoons extra virgin olive oil

2 medium onions, cut into thin wedges

2 red bell peppers, seeded and cut into thin wedges

2 cloves garlic, minced

1/4 cup chicken stock or water

1 1/4 cups orange juice

1 Tablespoon brown sugar

1 Tablespoon grapefruit juice

1 Tablespoon steak sauce

1 Tablespoon tamari

3 Tablespoons cornstarch

1 teaspoon orange zest

Directions:

Wash pork well under cold water. Trim fat from pork. Dry with paper towels.

In a small bowl, combine oregano, ginger, and pepper. Rub spice mixture over entire surface of meat. Place in a pan, cover with plastic wrap and refrigerate. This may be done up to 24 hours in advance.

In a large sauté pan, heat olive oil until hot but not smoking. Add pork and brown on all sides.

Transfer meat to slow cooker.

Add onions, red bell peppers and garlic to skillet. Cook 3 or 4 minutes. Transfer to slow cooker.

Add chicken stock to sauté pan; bring to boil and stir, scraping any brown bits off the pan. Pour into slow cooker.

In a bowl combine 1 cup orange juice, sugar, grapefruit juice, steak sauce, and tamari. Mix well and pour into slow cooker.

Cover and cook on Low for 8 to 10 hours or High for 4 to 5 hours.

Transfer roast to a serving platter; keep warm.

For sauce, measure pan juices into a heatproof measuring cup. Skim off fat. Add additional orange juice, if necessary, to make 2-1/4 cups.

In a medium saucepan combine cornstarch, remaining 1/4 cup orange juice, and orange zest; stir in reserved pan juices. Cook and stir until thickened and bubbly.

Cook and stir for 2 minutes more. Pass sauce with meat.

Nutritional Facts:

Serving Size: 1 (729 g)

Servings Per Recipe: 8

Amount Per Serving:

Calories 419.3	Sodium: 161.6 mg
Calories from Fat 205	Total Carbs: 11.6 g
Total Fat 22.8 g	Fiber: 0.6 g
Sat. Fat: 8.1 g	Sugars: 6.0 g
Cholesterol: 123.4 mg	Protein: 39.3 g

Pork Roast Sweet Potatoes and Onions

Total Time: 8 hrs. 30 mins.

Prep Time: 30 mins.

Cook Time: 8 hrs.

Servings: 9

Ingredients:

2 teaspoons fennel seeds, crushed

1 teaspoon dried oregano

1 teaspoon paprika

1 1/2 teaspoons garlic, chopped

1/2 teaspoon kosher salt

1/4 teaspoon freshly ground black pepper

2 Tablespoons extra virgin olive oil

2 lbs. pork loin roast, boneless

4 medium sweet potatoes, peeled and cut in half

1 large onion, peeled and cut in wedges

1 cup chicken stock or apple cider

Directions:

Wash pork well under cold water, dry with paper towels.

Combine fennel seeds, oregano, paprika, garlic, salt, and pepper.

Rub into pork.

Heat olive oil in a large skillet until hot but not smoking. Add pork and brown on all sides, about 10 minutes.

Place sweet potatoes and onions in slow cooker.

Transfer pork to slow cooker.

Add chicken broth to skillet and bring to a boil, stirring to loosen any browned bits that are stuck on the pan. Pour into slow cooker.

Cover and cook on Low for 8 to 10 hours.

Variation: Add baby carrots or peeled chunks of carrots to the sweet potatoes.

Apples are also a delicious addition to this dish. Core and chunk 2 or 3 cooking apples and mix them in with the sweet potatoes before adding pork.

Nutritional Facts:

Serving Size: 1 (187 g)

Servings Per Recipe: 9

Amount Per Serving:

Calories: 268.2	Sodium: 303.1 mg
Calories from Fat: 90	Carbs: 12.3 g
Total Fat: 10.0 g	Fiber: 2.0 g
Sat. Fat: 3.6 g	Sugars: 2.5 g
Cholesterol: 81.7 mg	Protein: 30.4 g

Dessert:

I grew up with a kitchen table which was 4' wide and 16' long and a mother who made wedding cakes. It was my job, until I turned 18 and left home, to scrape the piles and piles of frosting off the table several times a week. This exercise usually took place in the early morning hours because she would stay up all night to bake.

After breakfast was cooked and all the other morning chores were finished, I'd catch the bus to school. I still remember sitting at my desk and occasionally getting my hands too close to my face and the only thing I could smell was sugar.

Suffice it to say I don't crave sweets! ☺ I do enjoy a small bite or two occasionally.

Dessert isn't traditionally a part of the Mediterranean Diet. It's generally reserved for holidays and other special occasions. I've included a few of my favorites which aren't as sugar laden as some more traditional desserts.

Indian Pudding

Total Time: 2-3 hrs. or 6-8hrs. 30mins.

Prep Time: 5min.

Cook Time: 2-3 hrs. or 6-8 hrs.

Servings: 6

Served warm, this is a delicious sweet treat. Topped with a dollop of whipped cream, yogurt or ice cream, it's to die for! Try it, and it'll become one of your favorites too!

Ingredients:

3 cup milk

1/2 cup cornmeal

1/2 teaspoon kosher salt

3 eggs

1/4 cup light brown sugar

1/3 cup molasses

2 Tablespoons butter

1/2 teaspoon cinnamon

1/2 teaspoon ginger

2/3 cup chopped dates, raisins or dried cranberries, optional

Directions:

Lightly butter slow cooker. Preheat on High for 20 minutes.

In a large saucepan, bring milk, cornmeal and salt to a boil. Boil, stirring constantly, for 5 minutes. Reduce heat, cover and simmer an additional 10 minutes.

In a large bowl, combine eggs, brown sugar, molasses, butter, and spices.

Gradually beat hot cornmeal mixture into eggs, brown sugar mixture; whisk until smooth.

Stir in raisins, finely chopped dates or dried cranberries.

Pour into crock and cook on High for 2 to 3 hours or Low for 6 to 8 hours.

Nutrition Facts:

Serving Size 204 g

Amount Per Serving:

Calories: 296	Sat. Fat: 4.7g	Sodium: 322mg	Sugars : 34.2g
Calories from Fat:81	Trans Fat: 0.0g	Carbs :48.7g	Protein: 8.1g
Total Fat: 9.0g	Cholesterol: 102mg	Fiber: 2.5g	

Lemon Pudding Cake

Total Time: 2-3 hrs. 10 mins.

Prep Time: 10 mins.

Cook Time: 2-3 hrs.

Servings: 5-6

Ingredients:

3 eggs, separated

1 teaspoon grated lemon zest

1/4 cup fresh lemon juice

3 Tablespoons butter, melted

1 1/2 cups milk

3/4 cup sugar

1/4 cup flour

1/8 teaspoon kosher salt

Directions:

Butter the inside of slow cooker.

In a large bowl, beat egg whites until stiff peaks form. Set aside.

In a medium bowl, whisk egg yolks; blend in lemon juice, zest, butter and milk. Stir until just combined.

Combine sugar, flour and salt; add to egg –milk mixture, beating until smooth.

Fold into beaten whites.

Transfer to slow cooker.

Cover and cook on High for 2-3 hours.

Nutrition Facts:

Serving Size 158 g

Amount Per Serving:

Calories: 277	Sat. Fat: 6.2g	Carbs: 38.9g
Calories from Fat: 101	Cholesterol: 123mg	Sugars: 33.8g
Total Fat: 11.2g	Sodium: 181mg	Protein: 6.5g

Slow Cooker Baked Apples

Total Time: 2-3 hrs. 15 mins.

Prep Time: 15 mins.

Cook Time: 2-3 hrs.

Servings: 4

I usually substitute a couple tablespoons of pure maple syrup for the brown sugar and in the Fall I use non-preservative, non-pasteurized apple cider in place of apple juice or wine. Unfortunately, it's not available year round or in all parts of the country but its delicious if you can find it.

Ingredients:

4 large granny smith apples or cooking apples such as Cortland

1/3 cup firmly packed brown sugar

1/4 cup dried cranberries, raisins, dried cherries, dried blueberries or dried mixed fruit

1/2 cup dry white wine or 1/2 cup apple juice

2 Tablespoons butter, melted

1/2 teaspoon cinnamon

1/4 teaspoon nutmeg

1/2 cup chopped nuts or granola, as garnish

Directions:

Core apples.

In a medium bowl combine brown sugar and dried fruit and fill the centers of the apples with the sugar/fruit mixture.

Place the apples in slow cooker.

Combine the wine or apple juice with the melted butter and pour it over the apples.

Sprinkle the apples with cinnamon and nutmeg.

Cover slow cooker and cook on Low for 2 to 3 hours or until the apples are tender.

To serve, spoon the apples into individual dessert dishes, spoon juices over the apples, and sprinkle with chopped nuts.

Top with frozen yogurt, yogurt, ice cream or heavy cream.

Nutritional Facts:

Serving Size: 1 (301 g)

Servings Per Recipe: 4

Amount Per Serving:

Calories: 264.9	Sodium: 9.7 mg
Calories from Fat 55	Carbs: 50.6 g
Total Fat: 6.2 g	Fiber 5.8 g
Sat. Fat: 3.7 g	Sugars 41.5 g
Cholesterol: 15.2 mg	Protein 0.7 g

Brown Rice Pudding

Total Time: 4 hrs. 5 mins.

Prep Time: 5 mins.

Cook Time: 4 hrs.

Yield: 4 servings

Ingredients:

1/2 cup long-grain brown rice, jasmine rice or basmati rice

1 (14 oz.) can sweetened condensed milk

4 cups unsweetened coconut milk

2 teaspoons ground cinnamon

1/2 cup dried cranberries or raisins

Directions:

Lightly butter the slow cooker.

Combine all the ingredients in slow cooker, stirring well.

Cover, and cook on High for 3-5 hours or Low for 5-7 hours.

Serve topped with yogurt or whipped cream.

Nutritional Facts:

Serving Size: 1 (125 g)

Servings Per Recipe: 4

Amount Per Serving:

Calories: 108.2	Sodium: 133.3 mg
Calories from Fat: 2	Carbs.: 21.7 g
Total Fat 0.2 g	Fiber: 0.3 g
Sat. Fat: 0.1 g	Sugars: 0.0 g
Cholesterol: 1.2 mg	Protein: 3.9 g

Stewed Prunes

Total Time: 2-3 hrs. 3mins.

Prep Time: 3mins.

Cook Time: 2-3 hrs.

Serves: 6-8

Prunes make a nice simple week night dessert. They're also good for breakfast.

Ingredients:

1 (1lb.) package dried prunes (Sometimes sold as dried plums).

3 cups water

2 thin slices lemon

Directions:

Combine prunes with water. Add lemon slices. Cover and cook 2-3 hours on Low or until prunes are plump and tender.

Serve warm or cold.

Nutrition Facts:

Serving Size 76 g

Amount Per Serving:

Calories: 181	Cholesterol: 0mg	Fiber: 5.4g
Calories from Fat: 3	Sodium: 2mg	Sugars: 28.8g
Total Fat: 0.3g	Carbs: 48.3g	Protein: 1.6g

Thank You For Purchasing

I would appreciate it if you would leave a review for this book.

It not only tells others what you think,

It also tells me how I'm doing and what you need!

For a full explanation of the Mediterranean Diet check out my other book

The Mediterranean-Diet: The-Eating-Plan For A Healthy Life

Kate Rosetti